The Origins of Prejudice

Explanations in the Social Sciences

Explanations in the Social Sciences are short, authoritative books written by global scholars for students and the general public. Each volume explores a single question often asked about the demands and challenges of being human from an historical, as well as contemporary perspective. This series is designed to demonstrate how S.T.E.M. education must include the social sciences if we are to deal successfully with the risks and uncertainties of life today and in the future.

Volume 1
Sex, Risk, and Society: When Is It Dangerous?
Sarah H. Pollock

Volume 2
The Riddle of Intelligence: It's Not What You Think
John Terrell, Eugene Anderson, Foreman Bandama, Abhik Ghosh, and Marcia Leenen-Young

Volume 3
The Origins of Prejudice: Dangerous Opinions and Beliefs
Eugene Anderson, Kelley Coures, Carla Guerrón Montero, Tory Schendel-Vyvoda, Tobias Schwörer, and John Terrell

The Origins of Prejudice

Dangerous Opinions and Beliefs

Eugene Anderson, Kelley Coures, Carla Guerrón Montero,
Tory Schendel-Vyvoda, Tobias Schwörer, and John Terrell

berghahn
NEW YORK • OXFORD
www.berghahnbooks.com

First published in 2026 by
Berghahn Books
www.berghahnbooks.com

Library of Congress Cataloging-in-Publication Data

A C.I.P. cataloging record is available from the Library of Congress

British Library Cataloguing in Publication Data

A catalogue record for this book is available from the British Library

EU GPSR Authorized Representative

LOGOS EUROPE, 9 rue Nicolas Poussin, 17000, LA ROCHELLE, France
Email: Contact@logoseurope.eu

ISBN 978-1-83695-482-8 hardback
ISBN 978-1-80758-109-1 paperback
ISBN 978-1-83695-484-2 epub
ISBN 978-1-83695-483-5 web pdf

https://doi.org/10.3167/9781836954828

Contents

Figures

Introduction

The Nature of Prejudice

People and dogs are social creatures. We and they may be able to survive individually on our own, but we'd both rather not. In our case, it is doubtful how long most of us would be able to do so successfully.

Both dogs and people can be predators. We can be ready, willing, and able to hunt down and kill other creatures. In our case, those we kill (and, yes, sometimes eat) may even be others of our own kind (Siefkes 2022). Just as notably, we are also willing to kill as a form of entertainment. Whether dogs take pleasure in the act of killing is unknown, but certainly some people do find killing both thrilling and enjoyable. Unlike dogs, we are known to display the heads of those we kill as public witness to our evident prowess and worldly skill.

Furthermore, despite being remarkably social creatures, both dogs and people can develop personal likes and dislikes, fears , and avoidances. Yet despite their striking physical differences, dogs and people are not only able to get along well with one another, but may even develop deep affection for one another that we humans speak of as love.

If two creatures who are in many ways so different in their physical appearance and behavior can get along so famously, why are we as a species evidently so willing not only to favor our own likes and dislikes, fears and avoidances, but also act upon them in ways that can trivialize, demonize, exploit, and even lead to the death of others?

An Unfair and Unreasonable Opinion

Dictionaries generally agree on what the English word *prejudice* means. This is the term to use to talk about *an unfair and unreasonable opinion or feeling, especially when formed without enough thought or knowledge* ("prejudice").

Figure 0.1. Ten women and a little girl lined up for a bathing beauty contest, USA, 1920. Unnamed photographer for National Photo Company. Public domain, via Wikimedia Commons.

The German word for prejudice is *Vorurteil*. According to the philosopher Hans-Georg Gadamer, this word in German means "an unreflective judgment or over-hasty reasoning, resulting in bigotry of purely subjective opinion or the unreflective parroting of purely received wisdom" (Lawn and Keane 2011: 115). Similarly, back in 1764, the famous French philosopher Voltaire defined prejudice as "an opinion without judgment" in his *Philosophy Dictionary* (Cushing 2020: 27). Voltaire's definition, however, did not imply that prejudice is always a negative judgment, nor should this word only be used when you are talking about people.

Nowadays, according to Charles Sibley and Fiona Kate Barlow in *The Cambridge Handbook of the Psychology of Prejudice* (2017), it is conventional to think of prejudice as disliking whole groups or kinds of people. Given this, the social psychologists Robin Bergh and Mark Brandt (2022) have classified prejudice in the United States under three headings, or categories: "prejudice against marginalized groups, prejudice against privileged/conservative groups, and prejudice against unconventional groups." These bigoted or prejudiced hatreds of the "other" seem to be the contemporary, mainstream understanding of the word *prejudice*.

In 1954, the Harvard University professor Gordon Allport in *The Nature of Prejudice*—a book now widely recognized as a classic in the field of social psychology—focused attention on prejudice seen as a normal and understandable outcome of how we generally think about things and events as human beings. In particular, he defined ethnic prejudice as "an antipathy based upon a faulty and inflexible generalization. It may be felt or expressed. It may be directed toward a group as a whole, or toward an individual because he is a member of that group." He then added: "The net effect of prejudice, thus defined, is to place the object of prejudice at some disadvantage not merited by his own misconduct" (1954: 9).

In 1995, Stanley O. Gaines Jr. and Edward S. Reed critically observed that prejudice seen Allport's way "has its roots in the fallibility of the human perceptive or cognitive process that leads to 'thinking ill of others without sufficient warrant'" (1995: 97). They argued that prejudice viewed this way underplays the self-serving and intentional motivations that can be part of why we develop the prejudices we may act upon to the detriment of others.

Allport died in 1967. We cannot know how he would have replied to what Gaines and Reed wrote about his approach to understanding the roots of prejudice. In *The Nature of Prejudice*, he had been careful to offer several possible definitions of what this word means, starting with the one Gaines and Reed used in their critique: "Perhaps the briefest of all definitions of prejudice is: *thinking ill of others without sufficient warrant*" (Allport 1954: 6). He tells us that this definition, however, is too brief, although it includes what he saw as the two essential ingredients of all definitions of this word: "reference to unfounded judgment and to a feeling-tone."

Contrary to many definitions of this word—including the one by Allport just given—that are about negative prejudices, he was careful to note that our personal biases (he uses this word rather than *prejudice*) can be *pro* as well as *con*. Therefore, he suggested a better definition would be: "A feeling, favorable or unfavorable, toward a person or thing, prior to, or not based on, actual experience."

Allport emphasized that both of these definitions imply that our judgmental feelings are unwarranted whenever they lack a basis in fact. This may sound reasonable, and indeed many today would undoubtedly agree with the now-popular saying "facts matter." But what is a fact? And as he acknowledged: "It is not easy to say how much fact is required in order to justify a judgment. A prejudiced person will almost certainly claim that he has sufficient warrant for his views" (1954: 7).

Allport also observed that few if any human judgments are based on absolute certainty. Even so, he made a point of saying that a judgment is unwarranted whenever it lacks factual support. And it is precisely such judgments, he wrote—particularly those made about ethnic groups—that are rightfully labeled as prejudices rather than merely as opinions, biases, or what he favors calling "prejudgments":

> Here we have the test to help us distinguish between ordinary errors of prejudgment and prejudice. If a person is capable of rectifying his erroneous judgments in the light of new evidence he is not prejudiced. *Prejudgments become prejudices only if they are not reversible when exposed to new knowledge.* A prejudice, unlike a simple misconception, is actively resistant to all evidence that would unseat it. We tend to grow emotional when a prejudice is threatened with contradiction. Thus the difference between ordinary prejudgments and prejudice is that one can discuss and rectify a prejudgment without emotional resistance. (1954: 9)

Simple Definitions of *Prejudice*

(following Gordon Allport)

1. Thinking things that aren't true about other people.
2. Believing things that aren't true about groups of people.

Then What Is the Problem?

The Nature of Prejudice was published early in the Cold War following the defeat of Nazi Germany in 1945. Gordon Allport begins by first looking back briefly at what the world had then just been through less than a decade earlier. Despite our obvious mastery over energy, matter, and inanimate nature, he says, we are still living in the Stone Age when it comes to handling our human relationships. As prejudice in the United States alone shows unmistakably, although some of this endless antagonism may be based on genuine conflicts of interest, "most of it, we suspect, is a product of the fears of the imagination. Yet imaginary fears can cause real suffering" (Allport 1954: xiii).

Allport reassured his readers that not all is lost. "Especially encouraging is the fact that in recent years men in large numbers have become convinced that scientific intelligence may help us solve the conflict" between our human desires for peace and friendship, and our capacity for hatred, cruelty, and violence. "Let us make an objective study," therefore, "of conflict in culture and industry, between people of different color and race; let us seek out the roots of prejudice and find concrete means for implementing men's affiliative values." It took years of labor and billions of dollars, he reminds us, to crack the secret of the atom. "It will take a still greater investment to gain the secrets of man's irrational nature. It is easier, someone has said, to smash an atom than a prejudice."

Allport's enthusiasm seven decades ago for what the social sciences could do to save us from ourselves is unmistakable, although in this famous book his sights are only on clarifying the nature of prejudice. "But this issue is basic, for without knowledge of the roots of hostility we cannot hope to employ our intelligence effectively in controlling its destructiveness" (1954: xv).

Back then it certainly may have seemed reasonable and even self-evident to equate prejudice with ignorance and the worst characteristics of human nature. But what about our likes as well as our dislikes of people, things, and events? If liking vanilla ice cream or the music of Mozart rather than Bach aren't displays of prejudice, what then are such enthusiasms, biases, and predilections? Are our likes somehow fundamentally different from our dislikes? Are our predilections different from our prejudices? Are love and hate just two sides of the same coin, or are they really two fundamentally different ways of responding to people, and events . . . not to mention to dogs, cats, and other creatures?

We have more to say in the rest of this book about what Allport and others have said about dealing with the challenges of prejudice and human suffering. Before doing so, we want to offer you three examples showing that despite what has been written since the appearance of *The Nature of Prejudice*, the social sciences have not succeeded in doing what Allport forecast they would be able to do about the realities of prejudice.

Reasons for Doubt

As we will discuss again in Chapter 1, Allport mostly limited the scope of his study by focusing on prejudice defined as believing false claims about particular groups of people—he calls them "ethnic groups"—or individuals seen as belonging to such groups. He rejected the alternative claim that our attitudes about people are only to be seen as prejudiced if they violate local norms or values: "there is not the slightest justification for confusing the objective facts of prejudice with cultural or ethical judgment of these facts."

Having come down decidedly on the side of seeing prejudice as wrongfully judging other people, he confidently explains: "Some cultures, like our own, abjure prejudice; some do not; but the fundamental psychological analysis of prejudice is the same whether we are talking about Hindus, Navahos, the Greeks of antiquity, or Middletown, U.S.A. Whenever a negative attitude toward persons is sustained by a spurious overgeneralization we encounter the syndrome of prejudice. It is not essential that people deplore this syndrome. It has existed in all ages in every country. It constitutes a bona fide psychological problem. The degree of moral indignation engendered is irrelevant" (1954: 12).

If the word *prejudice*, however, just means having "a negative attitude toward persons" based on "spurious overgeneralization," so what? What is the problem? More to the point, what should we make of the following examples of attitudes and practices, all of which have consequences that are real enough even when they are not seen as reprehensible?

The Dog Meat Market

To those of us who dearly love our furry companions, the idea of eating them instead of pampering them is unthinkable. Not all of us, however, are vegans or vegetarians. Most of us have no trouble eating a pork chop, or a dish of creamy chicken pasta made with diced chicken, thick-cut bacon, artichoke hearts, and spinach. Such seemingly contradictory facts may not add up to what Allport called prejudice, but they do qualify as personal or ethical judgments. Moreover, pigs and chickens confined to a barnyard might noisily disagree if they had the power of speech and knew they were destined for the dinner table.

This is not a contrived (or cooked-up) example. It has been estimated that as many as thirty million dogs are killed for human consumption each year. Trade today in dog meat is widespread, particularly in China, South Korea, the Philippines, Thailand, Laos, Vietnam, Cambodia, Indonesia, and northern India. As reported by the Humane Society International, this trade is well organized. Dogs are often stolen or taken off the streets, transported over long distances, and brutally slaughtered ("Asian Dog Meat Trade").

Calling this trade a form of prejudice may seem farfetched. Looking more closely at the consequences suggests otherwise. According to FOUR PAWS, a global animal welfare organization founded in Vienna in 1988:

> Aside from the obvious animal welfare issues, the trade also poses a significant health risk to both animals and humans. There is an undeniable link between the dog meat trade and rabies, and it is simply incompatible with regional and global rabies elimination strategies. In many cases, the trade and slaughter of dogs and cats for consumption also operates in breach of existing national disease control and prevention legislation, and encourages other illegal activities such as pet theft, which is a growing societal problem in the region ("Dog Meat Market" 2020: 4).

Figure 0.2. Dogs destined to be eaten. © FOUR PAWS Organization, used by permission.

A Modest Proposal

Western biblical traditions of our Creation in the Garden of Eden tell us we are not like other creatures on Earth. We are uniquely different. We alone have souls and are capable of rational thought (Hatfield 2007, 2017). This helps explain why the French philosopher René Descartes (1596–1650) found it so meaningful to declare in 1637: "je pense, donc je suis" (I think, therefore I am). Since then, these words have been one of the foundational ideas of modern Western philosophy, although his declaration is usually rendered not in French but rather in Latin as *cogito, ergo sum* (Holyoak and Morrison 2011: 1).

Others, too, have done their best to draw a clear boundary line between us and other earthly life forms. According to the historian Esther Cohen at Hebrew University of Jerusalem: "Perhaps the most extreme expression of this approach was Descartes's idea, that animals are automata possessing neither sense nor feelings. Within this framework it was inconceivable that a beast should be placed in a human situation and treated as a human being" (1986: 16).

Descartes did not invent the idea of the soul, nor was he the first to grapple with the problem of how it is we are able to think about things that are not right there in front of us, to plot, to connive, and to wish even for unachievable rewards (Dennett 1988). To anyone, however, who has a much-loved family pet, the claim that animals other than ourselves cannot be thoughtful, loving, or hateful is incomprehensible. You might think, therefore, that favoring the companionship of family pets would mean being prejudiced also against eating other sorts of animals. Yet for many of us around the world, of course, this is not true, as a visit to any barnyard or slaughterhouse will attest. It may come as more of a surprise, however, that there is also no universal prejudice against the consumption of human flesh.

A Modest Proposal for Preventing the Children of Poor People in Ireland, from Being a Burden on Their Parents or Country, and for Making Them Beneficial to the Publick is a satirical essay written by Jonathan Swift (1667–1745) and first published anonymously in 1729. He suggests in this essay that those in Ireland who are poor should seriously consider selling their children to the rich to be eaten:

> I am assured by our merchants, that a boy or a girl, before twelve years old, is no saleable commodity, and even when they come to this age, they will not yield above three pounds, or three pounds and half a crown at most, on the exchange; which cannot turn to account either to the parents or kingdom, the charge of nutriments and rags having been at least four times that value.
>
> I shall now therefore humbly propose my own thoughts, which I hope will not be liable to the least objection.
>
> I have been assured by a very knowing American of my acquaintance in London, that a young healthy child well nursed, is, at a year old, a most delicious nourishing and wholesome food, whether stewed, roasted, baked, or boiled; and I make no doubt that it will equally serve in a fricasee [*sic*], or a ragoust. (Swift 1729)

Swift himself may not have wanted his proposal to be taken seriously. Rather, his intent was to ridicule those who were prejudiced in his day against the Irish and the poor of Ireland, who were predominantly of the Catholic faith. As Christian Siefkes (2022) has recently documented in much detail, however, history shows that human cannibalism—for instance, the capture and consumption of unwanted strangers and enslaved people—was decidedly a part of the slave trade in the colonialist history of Africa.

The Lynching of Robert Paul Prager

Seven months before the First World War ended when Germany surrendered to the Allied Powers on November 11, 1918, a German American named Robert Paul Prager was hanged from a tree shortly after midnight on April 5, 1918, in Collinsville, Illinois, while two hundred or so people watched (Schwartz 2002/2003). Born in 1886, Prager had immigrated to America in 1905. He was still a bachelor when he died. He had no relatives in the United States.

According to one commentator: "Shortly before his death he decided to become a miner, but his efforts to join the miners' union were unsuccessful, probably because he was an active socialist (it seems likely that his German birth was not the reason for his rejection since there were many German-Americans in the Collinsville area who were union members)" (Hickey 1969: 118). Apparently the union president had accused Prager of being a spy and a liar, charges he strongly denied. Nonetheless, on Thursday, April 4, he was seized by a group of miners and forced to kiss an American flag. Luckily, he had gotten away thereafter and was able to go back to his lodgings. But his luck soon turned. As this same historian relates: "This security was short-lived, however. In the evening a group of miners gathered at a saloon on the outskirts of Collinsville. They discussed the events which had occurred earlier in the day and the accusations which had been made against Prager. Most of the miners were foreign-born and spoke little English, and it is believed that comments imputed to Prager were magnified completely out of proportion. The result was that the miners decided Prager was disloyal to the United States and must be punished" (1969: 119).

There is apparently little doubt drinking far too much alcohol by those who finally lynched him is part of the explanation for what happened. Nevertheless, when American newspapers got word of this appalling event, editorials demanded that those responsible should be punished to the full extent of the law. As one editorial insisted, mob violence is "a species of collective criminality for which there is just one cure: punishment." The governor of Illinois at the time was also forthright in his condemnation of mob violence: "The action of the mob at Collinsville was as much an assault on the principle of democracy as the treasonable practices with which Prager was charged, even if that charge was true" (Hickey 1969: 123).

The leaders of the mob were arrested and held without bail pending grand jury action. Eleven men were finally brought to trial on May 13. The trial took three weeks. Seven hundred fifty men had been interviewed during the selection of the twelve men who were to finally determine the outcome. Those accused all denied responsibility for what had happened. They also did all they could to convince the jury that they were 100 percent American patriots.

After deliberating for just forty-five minutes, the jury returned a verdict of not guilty largely on the grounds that the lynching had been in a dark place, and hence ascertaining the identity of the actual perpetrators of the crime could not be done "beyond a reasonable doubt." Major newspapers around the country condemned this outcome as a gross miscarriage of justice.

Why did this lynching happen? The historian Earl Schwartz has a fairly convincing answer. "Prager unquestionably died at the hands of drunken, hysterical men because he was German. But when they killed Prager, they were also killing their own fears of being accused of disloyalty, fears rooted in a bitter and divisive labor struggle" (2002/2003: 414). Seeing this lynching as an example of the power of prejudice may seem too obvious to need mention. As noted earlier, Prager's execution was witnessed by at least two hundred people that night in 1918. If Schwartz is right, were they all experiencing more or less the same fear of being seen as unpatriotic during a time of war and labor unrest? Or were they seeing the event unfolding before their eyes through their own personal concerns, fears, and hatreds?

Rethinking Prejudice

Popular synonyms for *prejudice* suggest there is substantial agreement on the meaning of this everyday word (see box). When it is taken to mean self-serving thought and behavior that is often, but not always, ignorant and harmful to others, then the three examples just given can all be seen as differing illustrations of what is often labeled in this way. What is more debatable, however, is why anyone would act in such judgmental, prejudiced ways.

Synonyms for the word *prejudiced*

righteous, dogmatic, pigheaded, biased, bigoted, hostile, unfair, partisan, discriminatory, partial, one-sided, jaundiced, unjust, intolerant, narrow-minded, inequitable, nonobjective, distorted, unobjective, blinkered, partisan, predisposed, warped, loaded, weighted, chauvinistic, chauvinist, sexist, racist, opinionated, intolerant.

Perhaps the most popular explanation for why people can be prejudiced is indeed that we are all too willing to jump to conclusions without careful observation and thought. In keeping with this conventional idea, we were often told while we were writing this book that there is no mystery about why people are prejudiced: Just look at the word itself. Break it apart, and there you have the answer. Prejudice is *pre*judgment. As we will be discussing throughout the rest of this book, however, pulling this word apart does not explain why anyone would behave in such a fashion. And looking up dictionary definitions of the word *judgment* offers little useful help in unraveling why we can all be prejudiced from time to time—for example, judgment: *the ability to form valuable opinions and make good decisions* ("judgment").

The three historical and contemporary examples just given suggest a more useful explanation. As discussed in Chapter 3 using three case studies, it is possible to be prejudiced in astonishingly unpredictable ways. Nonetheless, there is something about human nature—about how we are naturally able to deal with the challenges of life—that can lead anyone to become prejudiced in one way or another. What we mean by the often-misunderstood phrase *human nature* will be discussed in some detail in Chapter 2.

Our Conclusions

The major conclusion about prejudice and human nature we offer you in this book is that prejudice should be defined in this way: *only seeing people, things, and events from your own point of view*. We have come to this conclusion for several reasons.

Prejudice Isn't an Explanation

Saying that *being prejudiced* shows you suffer from something called *prejudice* is an example of the logical error called the "fallacy of reification" (also known as the "fallacy of misplaced concreteness"). This fallacy is the blunder of mistaking something that is only a thought or an idea as something that is real, concrete, and even touchable. Classic examples would be the claim that someone does stupid things because they suffer from something called "stupidity." Or the claim that how intelligent you are depends on how much of something called "intelligence" you were lucky enough to be born with—perhaps in such abundance you can even be called a genius and compared with Albert Einstein. Or sadly, something you do not have nearly enough of, and so find yourself being seen by others, at least behind your back, as silly, stupid, or plainly idiotic.

Three Kinds of Prejudice

The human brain is not a computer, and prejudice is not a biologically inherited computer program lodged somewhere in your brain up there on your shoulders. As we discuss in some detail in the next two chapters, our prejudices are learned reactions and predilections. They are shaped and limited by how and what our senses are able to communicate to us. They are also shaped and honed by how we try to make sense of what we are picking up in this way from the outside world about people, things, and events happening around us. In this book, we call them *personal prejudices*. Furthermore, our prejudices are also informed by what others tell us about what is right or wrong, proper or improper, and so on. In this book, they are called *social prejudices*.

Both our own personal prejudices and our socially informed prejudices can have consequences for others if they lead us to act in ways that are either selfish or altruistic. If you hate someone, for instance, you may try to hurt or kill them. If you love someone, you may ask them to marry you.

As discussed in Chapter 1, our prejudices can also be *institutional prejudices*. As Stanley Gaines Jr. and Edward Reed wrote, despite Allport's fairly benign understanding of prejudice as the fallibility of human awareness, our prejudices can lead us to be selfish and self-serving not just when acting on our own but by ganging up with others—informally or in some formal way (e.g., by referendum or a show of hands)—to the detriment and even the survival of others. *Discrimination* is a word for behaving in this prejudiced way.

What is discrimination?

An assumption, claim, interpretation, categorization, labeling, etc. that is self-centered, inconsiderate, thoughtless, uncaring, insensitive, tactless, uncharitable, unkind, grasping, greedy, mercenary, or opportunistic

We Are Only Human

As we have already said in this chapter, Western biblical tradition tells us we are uniquely different from other creatures. The philosopher René Descartes not only went along with this claim but told us in no uncertain terms that we are the only creatures who are lucky enough to have souls, and therefore are the only ones able to think in rational ways.

However grand and wonderful such claims may sound, we are going to try to convince you that being prejudiced is a manifestation, a sign or symptom, of the fact that we are not as superior or godlike as we might wish to believe we are. In particular, and for understandable reasons, we have a hard time seeing things as other people see them, difficulty seeing things from their point of view. No wonder, therefore, we are sometimes—more often than we even realize—prejudiced to a fault.

Being so self-centered is not necessarily something we have to work at doing. Ironically, as highly social creatures, wanting to feel safe, secure, and in control can easily lead us to favor being with—or at least identifying with—others we believe are a lot like ourselves.

The Fallacy of the Group

A fallacy is an idea, a mistaken belief, that is widely taken to be true but is simply a deceptively bad argument ("fallacy"). One of the unexpected results of writing this book was discovering how widely accepted as true is the common belief that there are things out there in the real world variously called *groups*, *in-groups*, *out-groups*, *social groups*, and the like (e.g., Duckitt and Sibley 2017; Fiske 2012). We hope to convince you that this conventional belief is an example of the fallacy of misplaced concreteness. Groups can't have prejudices because they don't exist. As we explain in the Conclusion to this book, this does not mean that we cannot share our prejudices with others we live with, work with, or love. But there is a world of difference between using the little word *group* as a *noun* (as something in the real world) and as a *verb* (as in "to group" or "to create a grouping"—the latter confusingly also called "group").

As we will be saying repeatedly in this book, the human brain "groups" what we are experiencing in life to keep things and events as simple as possible and as memorable as may be needed as time goes by. Another less conventional word meaning "to group" is the verb "to categorize." This is a word we have already used in this chapter. We will be using it often in the chapters yet to follow.

What's Next

Here is a brief look at what you will find in the rest of this book. Chapter 1 explores three ways in which all of us can be prejudiced. Chapter 2 sets out how to unravel and try to understand the reasons, motivations, and real costs of being prejudiced. Chapter 3 offers three case studies of being prejudiced drawn from different places around the world to show

how challenging it can be to explain why people behave this way. In our Conclusion, we summarize the main issues we have discussed and offer practical suggestions on how to confront the social, economic, and practical costs of behaving in this way.

Key Points

1. People and dogs are strikingly different in their appearance and behavior, yet they are able to get along famously. Why are people, therefore, evidently so willing not only to favor their own likes and dislikes, fears and avoidances, but also can act in ways that trivialize, demonize, exploit, and may even lead to the death of others?
2. It is often said that the word *prejudice* means simply "prejudgment." This definition fails to explain why such judgments are made, or why they can be so dismissive, and even harmful.
3. There is something about human nature—about how we are naturally able to deal with the challenges of life—that can lead anyone to become prejudiced in one way or another.
4. Behaving in ways that are prejudiced can be intentional, self-serving, and clearly harmful to others.
5. We argue that prejudice should be defined in this way: *only seeing people, things, and events from your own point of view.*

1

Basic Questions

Figure 1.1. An example of institutional prejudice. *Stanley and the White Heroes in Africa; Being an Edition from Mr. Stanley's Late Personal Writings on the Emin Pasha Relief Expedition* (1890), page 358. Kelsey, D. M., [from old catalog] comp, No restrictions, via Wikimedia Commons.

"Halting at the village of Mbame, they were told that a slave party on its way to Tette would presently pass through. 'Shall we interfere?' they asked of each other. The question was a difficult one to answer, for all of their valuable goods had been left at Tette, and if they were to interfere to free these slaves, the owners of them might retaliate by procuring the destruction of these stores. But the slave-hunters had taken advantage of the expedition's opening the country to white men, and had persistently

> dogged their footsteps in places where they had never dared to venture before. The Englishmen therefore resolved to run all risks and put a stop, if possible, to the slave-trade, which had followed on the footsteps of their discoveries" (Kelsey 1890: 359–60).

As we said in the introduction, dictionary definitions and scholarly studies often give the impression that prejudice is an unfair yet basically blameless and perhaps unintentional error of human judgment motivated by ignorance, hearsay, and social conventions. At the start of this book, however, we offered you what we see as a better definition: *only seeing people, places, things, and events from your own point of view*.

Earlier we also proposed a longer definition of what can be called discrimination: *an assumption, claim, interpretation, categorization, labeling, etc., that is self-centered, inconsiderate, thoughtless, uncaring, insensitive, tactless, uncharitable, unkind, grasping, greedy, mercenary, or opportunistic*.

As helpful as they can be, however, definitions of prejudice are focused on answering the question *What?* They usually leave the *Why?* question unresolved, even unacknowledged.

How Are We Prejudiced?

Understanding what it means to be prejudiced can be harder to achieve than commonly acknowledged. Although an exhaustive survey of what has been written about prejudice is not possible in this short book—we do not discuss, for instance, evolutionary theories (Kenrick 2012)—there are common threads running through much of what has been said and claimed.

One common thread of, or possible reason for, why we can be prejudiced is the one Gordon Allport famously wrote about: How directly aware and well informed are you about other people and why they are doing what they are doing? There is no doubt, for instance, that trusting hearsay and modern social media too much can promote untruths and lead to misleading, even deadly, opinions and feelings about other people, places, and events.

Another and often-cited major cause of active prejudicial behavior—racism, religious bigotry, violence, and all—is the belief that life and the world is largely made up of zero-sum games: games in which someone wins and someone else loses by the same amount. Cross-cultural study goes on to reveal that the victims of serious prejudice and violence are not only not strangers—they are generally members of the best-known, longest-established, and most visible minority or minorities in the land.

A third common thread is the human need to feel in control of what is or could happen as we live our lives from day to day—the need all creatures have for an enduring sense of security, predictability, and confidence in their ways of dealing with the world and achieving their goals, however simple or elaborate they are (Langer 1983; Schulz 1976: 135–153). After all, building a nest to raise your young or building a skyscraper to house thousands may be orders of magnitude and complexity apart, but even so, they are basically alternative ways of accomplishing similar ends.

Another common thread is this one: thinking our own ways of doing things are the best ways to deal with other people, things, and events (Beck 1999). For example, politicians often claim they know how to fix popularly recognized economic problems (the cost of a dozen eggs, for example) and apparent social ills. But how practical, realistic, and honest are their claims and solutions?

Yet a fifth reason commonly given for why we can all be prejudiced at least sometimes is the idea that there is something "inside you"—an emotional feeling, bias, or conviction (Terrell and Terrell 2020: 106–107, 110–11, 118)—that for better or worse is causing you to see things more or less entirely from your own point of view (Seitz 2022; Seitz and Angel 2020; Seitz, Paloutzian, and Angel 2018; Terrell 2024). For example, being prejudiced is often described as a sign of being not just irrational but also truly hateful (Terrell 2015: 240–41).

Given these differing possible explanations, it seems clear that how to explain prejudice cannot be boiled down to a single reason or cause. Instead, prejudice can be seen as a mix of ingredients, so to speak, in differing proportions depending on the particulars of who, how, and why those involved are dealing with one another.

We have found that one way to describe this variable mix is to imagine someone has invented a device—perhaps inspired by virtual reality goggles—that lets us see what prejudice looks like when the "ingredients" are varied relative to one another.

The Virtual "Thought Slider"

Although a possibility that is more imaginary than practical or realistic, we find it useful to fantasize that the human brain is a secretive "thought slider," a fanciful kind of tool comparable to the color sliders found in paint stores and online. Color sliders make it possible for you to see what you'd get if you mixed together three primary colors—red, blue, and green—in different amounts to create the perfect color you have in mind, say, for your bedroom, kitchen, hallway, and the like (Figure 1.2, top).

Similarly, the thoughts—and beliefs—jostling for your attention up there in your head can also be described as a mix of similarly basic ingredients. As shown in Figure 1.2 (bottom), the three "mental ingredients" we have in mind are:

1. *Intent*: the reason or reasons you have for wanting to do, or not do, something ranging from those that are purely random and unintentional to reasons that are totally deliberate and intentional.
2. *Ability*: how successfully you may be able to do something to achieve what you have in mind, ranging from "not a chance, buddy!" to gaining total control and complete mastery.
3. *Knowledge*: how well you know what is happening and might be done to achieve whatever it is you want to accomplish, ranging from delusional fantasy to something that you totally get and fully understand. Between these two extremes are what you only indirectly learn about from others through hearsay, gossip, social media, and the like—all of which may mislead you and even result in total failure.

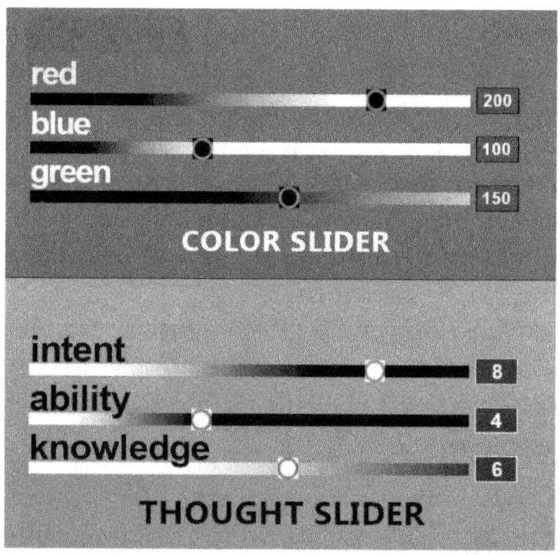

Figure 1.2. (top) Black-and-white version of a sliding color picker used to blend together in different amounts three basic colors (red, blue, and green) to create a desired result. The button on each of the three sliders controls the saturation level of that particular color ranging from 0 (none) to 255 (full saturation). (bottom) Our fanciful "thought slider" modeled on this color picker illustrating how thoughts and actions can vary depending on (a) how deliberately "between 1 and 10" you are doing something (*intent*), (b) how well you can do it (*ability*), and (c) how informed you are about what is happening (or could happen) and why (*knowledge*). © John Edward Terrell

Three Kinds of Prejudice

Just as a color slider shows you the color you will get depending on the saturation level you give each of the three basic colors used, so too, our imaginary thought slider is a way to think about the thoughts and prejudices you have—perhaps without realizing it—created by (1) how deliberately you want to do something (*intent*), (2) how well you are able to do whatever it is you have decided to do (*ability*), and (3) how well you understand what you are dealing with (*knowledge*).

To make this imaginary thought slider more realistic, consider these three examples, each of which takes it more or less for granted that you want to control what is happening around you, but you may not necessarily be able to know and understand what it takes to succeed. The three categories used are those first proposed in the opening chapter in this book (page 12).

Personal Prejudice

> How you feel about other people, places, and events, and what you are willing to do.

Uncle Tom's Cabin was written by the abolitionist Harriet Beecher Stowe (1811–1896). Hundreds of thousands of copies of this book were sold in the months immediately following its publication in two volumes in 1852. Despite its popularity, this work of fiction has been both praised for its depiction of the evils of slavery before the Civil War, and also vilified for its sentimentalism and stereotypic characterizations of Black Americans. As the British journalist J. C. Furnas noted in 1956 in his book *Goodbye to Uncle Tom*, African Americans have made the term "Uncle Tom" "a hissing and a byword," and many would rather be called "nigger" than "Uncle Tom" (Dinerstein 2009: 87).

In the years leading up to the Civil War, the Black abolitionist Frederick Douglass was a highly visible and much-respected voice against slavery. In the same year that *Uncle Tom's Cabin* first appeared in serial form (1851), he began weekly publication of a four-page newspaper, *Frederick Douglass' Paper*. Stowe's book was first mentioned on its pages in a review published on April 8, 1852. Although it was a short review, the sentiments Douglass expressed are obvious. "The friends of freedom owe the Authoress a large debt of gratitude for this essential service rendered by her to the cause they love."

Douglass and Stowe knew and worked with one another. History tells us that both of these influential abolitionist voices, one a White woman and the other a Black man, genuinely believed all Americans should and must be free (Levine 1992: 81–82). Other Black leaders and intellectuals in the middle of the nineteenth century, however, did not share the belief that "our white friends" could or should play decisive roles in the advancement of Black Americans. Moreover, as Robert Levine at the University of Maryland observed in 1992, Douglass and Stowe may have shared the same beliefs about slavery but they did not share the same underlying assumptions about what Black people are capable of achieving.

Like many then, both White and Black, Stowe took the assumption as more or less self-evident that Black people and White people are fundamentally different kinds of human beings belonging to distinctly different human races (Armbruster 2023). Douglass evidently also shared this widely accepted idea. According to Robert Levine, the difference between them was that Douglass also believed that Black Americans are entirely capable of uplifting themselves.

After the Civil War, Stowe's racial and political views changed in keeping with postwar sentiments in the North, leading to the widespread acceptance of racial discrimination in America during the period of Reconstruction. Instead of working to educate and integrate emancipated Black Americans, she promoted the view that they are by their very nature "laborers of the tropical regions" who are not only immensely strong but thrive and flourish "under a temperature that exposes a White man to disease and death" (quoted in Armbruster 2023: 2–3). Put simply, Stowe became a full-fledged White American racist. Their compatible, yet also contradictory, reasons and motivations may explain, at least in part, why Frederick Douglass and Harriet Beecher Stowe evidently saw eye to eye on the evils of Black slavery in the United States, but not about the basic equality of Black people and White people.

On our virtual thought slider, therefore, we would certainly rate both Douglass and Stowe—on a scale from 1 to 10—as (a) unquestionably high on *intent*, (b) fairly low on their *ability* to change the world to meet their visionary goals (moreover, surely not equally low), but (c) at best only moderately "as of one mind," to use the familiar phrase for sharing the same beliefs and *knowledgeable* understandings.

Such conflicting motivations are still very much part of life and politics today, just as they were more than a hundred seventy-five years ago (Kanai and Gill 2020). We are similarly living during a time of marked social and political upheaval, this time around popularly called "wokeness," a time when issues of gender and sexuality as well as race are prominent in the press, in online social media, and during political campaigns.

Social Prejudice

What you think about other people, places, and events you have learned from other people.

In our opening chapter, we discussed how influential Gordon Allport's 1954 book *The Nature of Prejudice* has been in the study and understanding of prejudice. The social psychologist Irwin Katz in 1991 left no doubt about his own appraisal of this singular book, which, he observed, "remains one of the most influential and often-cited publications in the entire field of intergroup relations" (1991: 125). In 2014, the social psychologist Thomas Pettigrew—an expert on American civil rights, race, and ethnic inequality—and his colleague Kerstin Hammann praised this book for its "seamless and vigorous perspective."

> *The Nature of Prejudice* is probably the most read volume in the history of social psychology. Translated into multiple languages, the volume met two quite different needs. First, it organized and structured the study of intergroup prejudice for the next half-century. . . . Especially impressive is how many of Allport's contentions have been supported by intensive research during the past half-century. . . . Second, the book had a significant impact on popular thinking. It was simply written, making it accessible to the general reader. (Pettigrew and Hammann 2014: 174)

We agree that Allport's book has all but defined for decades social psychology's understanding of prejudice as a group phenomenon manifest most tellingly in ethnic (and racial) conflicts and social inequality. In the book you are now reading, however, we want to underscore two things.

First, prejudice is not just a group phenomenon. As we have already remarked in the Introduction, Allport himself defined prejudice in several ways. Perhaps his most widely accepted definition, however, is how he explained ethnic prejudice as "an antipathy based upon a faulty and inflexible generalization. It may be felt or expressed. It may be directed toward a group as a whole, or toward an individual because he is a member of that group." Recall that he then added: "The net effect of prejudice, thus defined, is to place the object of prejudice at some disadvantage not merited by his own misconduct" (1954: 9). He was well aware, nevertheless, that all of us have individual thoughts and prejudices, and our prejudices are not always negative ones (6).

Second, prejudice is an all-too-easy by-product, so to speak, of how we all deal with the world around us—and not just other people—in ways that can be far from realistic or kind. As Pettigrew and Hammann have remarked, Allport fully acknowledged that "cognitive factors, and cognitive considerations" are a key element in the formation of our prejudices, social and otherwise (Pettigrew and Hammann 2014: 195).

Nonetheless, as Irwin Katz (1991) as well as Stanley Gaines Jr. and Edward Reed (see Introduction, page 3, 12) have observed, Allport's focus on stereotyping and socially acquired negative attitudes and beliefs about recognized groups underplays the self-serving motivations behind what people think about other people, and about what is or is not possible or acceptable in the world around them.

Allport's own interest in pinning down the social reasons for why people are prejudiced was commonly shared by other social scientists back then, as it still is today. As Patrick Schmidt (2022) has documented, he was one of the leading scholars of his day who tried after World War II to promote cultural anthropology, sociology, clinical psychology, and social psychology collectively as a "new science." At Harvard University, he was one of the prime advocates for the establishment of a new department there dedicated to proving the hopeful claim that interdisciplinary research in the social sciences was the wave of the future. Such a department at Harvard had been years in the making. Finally, it was formally created by the Faculty of Arts and Sciences on January 29, 1946. At 5:59 that same afternoon it was given the name "Department of Social Relations," or, as it was to become known by students and others there, "Soc Rel."

For reasons that we will not go into here, the credibility of this new science was never firmly established at Harvard or elsewhere. Gordon Allport was one of the founders of this department. Perhaps not surprisingly, in 1968 he saw the problems it was dealing with as a viable department at Harvard as institutional—that is, as social. Schmidt has quoted him directly: "The problem of the department has been to balance the needs of specialization with a measure of desired cross-disciplinary training. Our policies have followed a wavering course between specialism and integrationism, with no satisfactory proportion yet discovered" (2022: 162).

From our perspective on the nature of prejudice, however, at least part of the problem was that this seemingly promising academic undertaking failed to address successfully enough that the issues we all face as human beings are not always or simply social. Allport himself was well aware of the psychological and motivational dimensions of success or failure. As Gaines and Reed have said, however, he was not attentive enough to the cold realities of our success or failure both as individuals and as a species.

Therefore, once again using our virtual thought slider, when it comes to socially acquired prejudices, (1) how invested you are in them may have little to do with what you yourself want and believe, (2) how much time and effort you are willing to put into achieving what they are about may depend mostly on how much you want to "go along with the crowd," and

(3) you may not need to know all that much about why other people have the prejudices they evidently have—a "monkey see, monkey do" explanation for why we can be prejudiced that doesn't say much for our critical skills and concerns.

Institutional Prejudice

What people are allowed to do by other people depending on how they are socially categorized and labeled.

One of the challenges of being born human is that there is often, maybe almost always, more than one way to do something. So, who decides? People who get to be called parents? Those socially identifiable as experts who are called scientists, doctors, politicians, or preachers? Who?

For instance, the country known today as Afghanistan in Central Asia is geographically dominated by the rugged Hindu Kush mountain range. Historically once a major center of Buddhism, Afghanistan today is, and has always been, an environmentally demanding place to call home. To make life there even more challenging, this is a land that has long been a well-traveled route across Asia and a social world often dominated by foreigners.

While both personal and social prejudice focus on how all of us interpret, categorize, and label ourselves, other people, and events as a routine part of life, *institutional prejudice* imposes a set of rules, regulations, and requirements on people that not everyone may believe in or want to accept.

The Taliban (a word meaning "students") became a major political force in Afghanistan in the 1990s. Their goal was to restore security, stability, and prosperity to this landlocked country while enforcing their own strict interpretation of Islamic law (Humans Rights Watch n.d.). Between 1996 and 2001 they ruled much of this mountainous country until they were overthrown by an American-led invasion. After two decades of insurgency, however, they regained control in 2021 following the departure of the governing foreign coalition forces. They restored their constitution, which identifies Islam as the national religion.

Under the Taliban's rule, the public has minimal involvement in decision-making and lacks voting rights. Moreover, the Taliban's extreme interpretation of Islamic Law restricts women from pursuing education or working outside their homes. They must adhere to a stringent dress code (Fair Observer 2022). Additionally, the Taliban interpretation of Islamic Law has led to the removal of non-Islamic symbols, most famously the two Bamiyan Buddhas shown in Figure 1.3. As the Taliban's supreme leader Mullah Mohammad Omar stated in 2001: "These idols [the Bamiyan Buddhas] have been gods of the infidels." He ordered their removal (Tristam n.d.).

Figure 1.3. (left) The larger of the two Bamiyan Buddhas in 1936. These monumental statues 115 and 174 feet tall were carved around the sixth century in the sandstone cliffs of the Bamiyan Valley of central Afghanistan. Frederick Gardner Clapp, Public domain, via Wikimedia Commons. (right) All that was left of the largest of these two statues after their demolition in March 2001 at the hands of the Taliban. UNESCO, CC BY-SA 3.0 IGO, via Wikimedia Commons.

Under the Taliban regime, the impact of their way of seeing what is and isn't acceptable has consequences throughout Afghanistan. For example, the family of Bibi Nazdana promised when she was seven that she would marry Hekmatullah "to turn a family *enemy* into a *friend*" (Durrani and Khamoosh 2024). When she was fifteen, Hekmatullah asked that this promise be fulfilled. It did not take long, however, for Bibi's family to realize this had become a bad marriage. Bibi, with the support of her brother, Nazdana, filed for divorce. She won her case for separation. But then Bibi's divorce was overturned in 2024, and so have tens of thousands of others. As reported in 2024 by Mamoon Durrani from the BBC Afghan Service, and Kawoon Khamoosh from the BBC World Service, one can find Bibi now living on the streets, clutching her divorce papers, hoping someone will help her.

The policies detailed in the Taliban's constitution affect men as well as women. They are forbidden, for example, from helping women oppose the policies affecting them, some of which seem undeniably prejudiced when seen from a more global perspective. For example, women and girls today in Afghanistan are banned from attending secondary school (equivalent to middle school in the United States) and are forbidden from attending university. Even with the approval of her father, if a woman attends school without proper approval, the family may be held responsible, as reported by a fifteen-year-old girl from Kabul in 1995: "They shot my father right in front of me. It was nine o'clock at night. They came to our house and told him they had orders to kill him because he allowed me to go to school. The Mujahideen [Taliban] had already stopped me from going to school, but that was not enough. I cannot describe what they did to me after killing my father" (Amnesty International 2023). In December 2024, the Taliban further restricted women's educational opportunities by banning them from training as nurses and midwives, a right that women previously had since women are unauthorized to be treated or seen by male healthcare professionals or doctors (Kumar and Joya 2024).

When seen using our imaginary thought slider, life in Afghanistan today comes across as an extreme example of institutionalized prejudice. The Taliban are more than just arguably high on all three of the dimensions we have used—*intent*, *ability*, and *knowledge*. They say they are doing what they say must be done according to their constitution and their interpretation of Islamic Law. According to news reports, however, what women there may and may not do also depends on motives that are not religious or lawful. A spokesman for the Taliban government has explained that, to men like himself, even a fully covered woman can be sexually arousing. "Seeing women working in kitchens, in courtyards or collecting water from wells can lead to obscene acts" (Bennett 2025). The irony here is that when you use a color slider, maximizing all three colors results in the color white. Evidently, maximizing restrictions on what women today can do in Afghanistan is thought to maximize the purity of being colorless.

But Is It Really Prejudice?

In 2004, the journalist David Corn wrote a highly critical commentary about another journalist named William Safire who had then recently written about Islamic extremism and political intrigues in war-torn Iraq (Corn 2004). The issue motivating his remarks was whether Safire, or any other columnist, was "free to make a false assertion and not have to correct it?"

Corn's critique of what Safire had reported is well worth reading. Here we only want to note how Corn in his commentary defined the familiar word *opinion* using a quotation from yet another political journalist, Elizabeth Drew, to support how he favors doing so. "Opinion *n. 1. A belief or conclusion held with confidence but not substantiated by positive knowledge or proof.* 'The world is not run by thought, nor by imagination, but by opinion.' *(Elizabeth Drew).*" Dictionaries basically agree with Corn's definition, which also sounds a lot like conventional definitions of the word *prejudice.*

As we noted at the start of this book, Gordon Allport knew it is not easy to say how much fact is required to justify a prejudice. To quote him again: "A prejudiced person will almost certainly claim that he has sufficient warrant for his views." Trying to decide, therefore, whether to call something an opinion or a prejudice may ironically just be a matter of opinion. We think it is possible to draw two important conclusions from this observation:

1. Instead of trying to decide whether any given opinion or prejudice is true or false, what needs to be determined instead is what are the likely *consequences* of believing the claims being made. Are the consequences acceptable or not?
2. As life today in Afghanistan under the militant Taliban shows us, one of the characteristics of institutional prejudice is the use and enforcement of publicly announced rules and regulations. As we will discuss in greater detail in the final chapter of this book, this does not mean, however, that everyone believes in and accepts these rules and regulations.

Therefore, call them opinions, prejudices, or religiously inspired truths; surely what matters is not how we label them, but instead what are the consequences of living with, or having to live by, such dictates and directives.

The Color of Prejudice

Definitions of prejudice commonly explain such self-centered thinking by saying such thoughts are colored by having too little of the top and bottom ingredients on our imaginary thought slider—*intent* and *knowledge*—in the mental mix. When explained this way, the solution to prejudice would seem simple. All we need to do is take the time and make the effort to add more knowledge. Then all will be fair and well.

We think the three examples discussed in this chapter show why such a seemingly blameless explanation for thoughts and deeds that can be justifiably called prejudiced is wishful thinking. Why do we say this so assuredly? Prejudice can be understood best as a combination, or mix, of these mental ingredients:

1. How intentionally we *want* to achieve our goals and objectives,
2. How we *can* achieve what we want, perhaps by any means including violence and bloodshed, and
3. What we *know*, or do not know, about both the situations we are dealing with and what other people may want to have or achieve in life.

When seen this way, being prejudiced clearly involves more than just being lazy, hasty, and unobservant. In the next chapter, we describe ways in which it may be possible to sort out and decide what combinations of these ingredients can be used to best account for the specific prejudices you want to get to understand and explain.

Key Points

1. Understanding what it means to be prejudiced can be harder than commonly acknowledged.
2. One of the challenges of being human is that there is often more than one way to do something. So, who decides what should be done?
3. Instead of arguing about whether prejudices are right or wrong, it makes sense to ask whether the consequences are acceptable. If so, why?

2

Possible Answers

Figure 2.1. The categorization of human beings by their physical appearance and working relationship (or function). Yale Varsity rowing lineup (between ca. 1910 and 1915), Bain News Service. Library of Congress, No restrictions, via Wikimedia Commons.

In Chapter 1, we described three differing sorts of prejudice: personal prejudice, social prejudice, and institutional prejudice. Although we did not say so then, personal prejudice basically involves both grouping (that is, *categorization*) and grading (*classification*). People, things, and events are labeled and judged as good or bad, acceptable or not, likable or not, and so forth. Social prejudice adds to this way of developing our personal feelings and judgmental opinions. This type of prejudice builds on how others, too, label and evaluate what people, things, etc., can do, or should be permitted to do, and so forth. Institutional prejudice takes this sort of discrimination to a more publicly codified and enforceable level. Institutional prejudice is not just about feelings and opinions but about demands and requirements.

When the topic for discussion, however, is not just what is prejudice as a way of dealing with the world, but also what are prejudices, it soon becomes obvious that almost anything about the world and our being in it can be turned into a prejudice. The anthropologist R. S. Khare, for example, has compared the caste system of India to a cobweb. He has argued that thinking about how people deal with one another in India in this metaphorical fashion captures the insidious, elusive, and complex ways of this long-established method of ordering who can and cannot do this or that or something else based on the circumstances of their birth (Pandey 2013: 83).

But this, too, is certain. The caste system of India is only one of the seemingly countless ways in which characteristics of who we are, what we look like, where we are, and so on can be and have been used to determine what can and cannot happen over the course of an individual's time on earth. Examples of other characteristics, real or imagined, include ideas about race, ethnicity, gender, sexual identification, economy, or religion. Said more directly, the prejudices we humans have are not simply black-or-white "pre-judgments" about something or someone as good or bad. Our prejudices are like cobwebs that build up over time even while we may not be paying attention to what is happening and why.

Analyzing Prejudice

The word *prejudice* is only one of a number of words in the English language used to talk about our settled ways—our conventional *attitudes*—for handling people, things, and events. Other examples would be these: *belligerent*, *hateful*, *warm-hearted*, *loving*, *long-suffering*, *easy-going*, and the like.

As we have already said, Gordon Allport's chief explanation for why we all develop attitudes such as these is to credit, or rather blame, our supposed willingness to model our behavior and feelings on what we see others doing immediately around us. "Everywhere on earth we find a condition of separateness among groups. People mate with their own kind. They eat, play, reside in homogeneous clusters. They visit with their own kind, and prefer to worship together. Much of this automatic cohesion is due to nothing more than convenience" (Allport 1954: 17).

Accepting this argument, and given the purported ignorance born of social isolation, it might seem easy to explain how our attitudes and feelings about other people—particularly negative ones about those who come across to us as strangely different from people we know nearby—are easily acquired as a normal part of our daily lives. "The initial fact, therefore, is that human groups tend to stay apart. We need not ascribe this tendency to a gregarious instinct, to a 'consciousness of kind,' or to prejudice. The fact is adequately explained by the principles of ease, least effort, congeniality, and pride in one's own culture" (Allport 1954: 19).

Perhaps Allport was right, but why blame isolation and something called "culture" as the leading causes of prejudice, or even just negative prejudice? Instead, as a working proposition, it seems wise to keep in mind that how we are likely to respond to people, things, and events—our attitudes toward our experiences in life—can be formed, shaped, and modified by more than just who we come into contact with and how we encounter others from one day to the next. Again, as a working proposition, our own personal experiences as well as our other beliefs and intentions surely also need to be considered.

The virtual thought slider we introduced in Chapter 1 (Figure 1.2) as a way to model how complicated human thinking about anything can become may be used to analyze how challenging it can be to understand and explain why anyone does anything, however good, bad, or vitally necessary. The "colors" of the three bars on our thought slider are labeled *intent*, *ability*, and *knowledge*. But an even more basic way of labeling these three dimensions of our thought slider is to call them *want*, *can*, and *know*.

Journalism students have long been taught that there are six questions to ask whenever you are trying to understand and report on current events: *when*, *where*, *who*, *what*, *how*, and *why*? All these questions can be asked not only about the news of the day but also about what it means to be prejudiced.

The questions when, where, and who? are often asked about history and human evolution. We call them the journalist's three standard "historical questions." We call the other three—what, how, and why?—the "hard questions" of cause and effect.

We have found it helpful to combine the three "colors" on our thought slider with these three similarly basic questions. This seemingly farfetched way of using all six to come to grips with prejudice has been inspired by the usefulness of what is popularly called SWOT analysis (Figure 2.2,

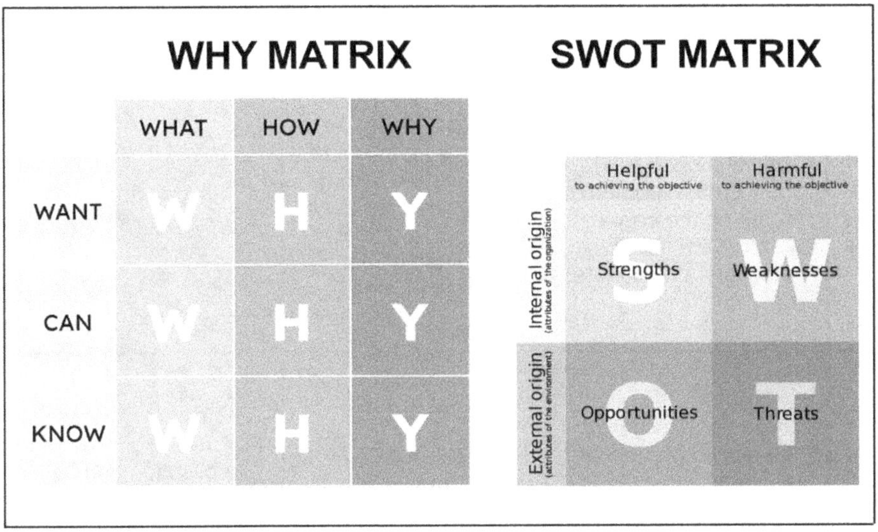

Figure 2.2. (left) A WHY Matrix. Each of the three questions at the top should be asked about each of the desires and abilities listed in the left-hand column. For example, what do you want? How do you think it can happen? Why do you want it to happen? (right) A standard SWOT Matrix to be completed to help identify and analyze the internal and external factors that may have an impact on a project, product, place, or person you want to manage successfully. SWOT Mastrix: Xhienne, CC BY-SA 2.5, via Wikimedia Commons ©John Edward Terrell

right), a strategic planning tool used in the business world to model and analyze the *strengths*, *weaknesses*, *opportunities*, and *threats* you need to face and try to deal with if you want to succeed in the real world.

Although this particular strategy for seeing what can be done to achieve worthy (and hopefully lucrative) corporate goals was developed in the competitive world of business and industry, this elementary approach to decision-making is now widely seen as a useful way to pin down the internal and external factors that may determine the success of a project or product in the commercial world (Puyt et al. 2020). What is called "doing a SWOT," however, is just a fancy name for filling out as best you can the four cells of what is known in statistics and the sciences as a 2 x 2 table.

Our WHY Matrix has nine cells rather than four (Figure 2.2, left). It asks you to answer the three questions listed on the left side about what, how, and why (a) you want to do something, (b) may be able to do something, and (c) may know enough about what the likely result would be if you were to do it.

	WHAT	HOW	WHY
WANT	I want a dog. Definitely not a cat. Cats scratch furniture. Vomit on the carpet. Must have a litter box. Aren't very affectionate.	I want to adopt an older dog from an animal rescue that has given it medical care and kept it safe until I can give it a "forever home."	I love dogs, and I am lonely.
CAN	There are two animal rescue organizations near me were I can adopt a dog.	I can make appointments to visit these animal rescue organizations.	I will need to fill out an application and be approved as a forever home before I can adopt my dog.
KNOW	I have found pictures on their web pages of some really cute dogs needing placement in forever homes.	I know my application to adopt my dog must be approved by the animal rescue organization, and I will need to pay an adoption fee.	I realize that my application to adopt a dog could be turned down by the rescue organization if they think I cannot give it a good home.

Figure 2.3. This simple example of WHY Analysis shows how "thinking about things" even when you are prejudiced in favor of dogs rather than cats calls for knowing and thinking about a wide range of interrelated facts, figures, and events. © John Edward Terrell

The Problem with Prejudice

The psychologist John Dovidio and his colleagues observed in 2005 that Allport himself did not advocate for a particular theory of prejudice, and instead surveyed a variety of ways to think about this topic. As anyone who reads *The Nature of Prejudice* soon discovers, he also appears to favor seemingly contradictory views at different places during his challenging analysis. "For example, Allport is the founder of the cognitive approach to prejudice, which views stereotyping and categorization as normal and inevitable by-products of how people think. Yet he also viewed prejudice as a fundamentally irrational hatred, born of ignorance and the ego-defensive maneuvers of people with weak personality structures" (Dovidio et al. 2005: 1–2).

Dovidio and his colleagues attribute the seeming inconsistency of Allport's survey partly to the complexity of prejudice as a phenomenon. As discussed in Chapter 1, this is not an unreasonable explanation, although this might be said about almost any topic that is given serious and prolonged study. At least part of the apparent complexity, however, of figuring out what is or isn't prejudice is due to the fact that prejudice isn't just one thing, and it isn't even a thing. Rather, as we suggested at the beginning of this book, this is a word commonly used to describe how we are all prone to see things not only from our own point of view but also for our own reasons.

There is no doubt, for instance, that ignorance and hearsay can sometimes lead to prejudice. How frightening or sweetly appealing, for example, a dog may seem can be based on little more than their appearance. Dogs labeled for this reason as "pit bulls" were once seen as wonderfully compliant companions for small children. Nowadays, they are commonly described instead as dangerous animals that are extremely capricious in their behavior (Figure 2.4).

What is important is whether there is a way to deal with such prejudice. According to the clinical psychologist Adam Duberstein and his colleagues, "With training in both animal and human behavior, psychologists have a special mandate to educate the public that these dogs are no more likely to do harm than any other type of canine. By using their education to advocate for these animals and the humans who care about them, psychologists can improve mental health outcomes both for dogs and for the humans who love them" (2023: 183).

This strikes us as good advice, but don't overlook that prejudice can be an intentional manipulative strategy designed to advance our own interests over the welfare and even the survival of others, dogs included. Moreover, the motivations behind putting our own self-interests above the interests of others may be secretly personal or quite public. There is no doubt, for instance, that hostility toward others may be due to a sense of vain rivalry, or to existential fears about losing control over valued resources or the labor of others.

By using all nine of the analytical cells in our WHY Matrix, it may be easier to see that prejudice can be a problem that cannot easily be resolved or overcome by education and advocacy. The prejudices we have can be excuses for *what*, *how*, and *why* we want something regardless how our own wants may conflict with those of others near or far.

Figure 2.4. How a dog is identified as belonging to a particular type, or "breed," may determine how they are believed to behave. According to Adam Duberstein and his colleagues, "pit-bull-type dogs in high-kill shelters run an increased risk of being murdered simply due to no reason other than their blocky-headed appearance" (Duberstein et al. 2023). Actual experience with dogs, however, is usually needed before deciding whether what is believed about them is true. Three of these pictures are of the same dog (her name is Emma) who is often identified by strangers as a "pit bull." This label, however, is commonly used for a variety of dogs of similarly solid, muscular appearance. And yes, she has incredibly impressive jaws. Upper left: An angry dog. Rawpixel, CC0 1.0, Public domain. Bottom: A hostile dog, from Charles Darwin's *The Expression of the Emotions in Man and Animals*, 1873. Wellcome Trust, CC BY 4.0, via Wikimedia Commons. © John Edward Terrell

Evidence Not Required

However faulty or truthful they are, and however unbiased or prejudiced they may be, our assumptions and beliefs about life and the world around us are commonly formed in more or less the same way. Here is one example.

As shown in Figure 2.5, it has long been a common belief that wolves are dangerous despite the fact that the risk posed by wolves is so small the evidence for such a claim cannot even be calculated. It is true that history shows wolf attacks have repeatedly occurred throughout the last four hundred years in Europe. New understanding of wolves in recent years, however, has "simply brought wolves into the same frames that we use to consider the potential risks posed by all large predators, like polar, black, brown and sloth bears, lions, tigers, leopards and cougars, and sharks and crocodiles" (Linnell et al. 2021: 10). Statistically, moreover, all of these listed predators are less dangerous than our fellow human beings can be.

More to the point, the fear that wolves are dangerous is unlikely to be based on our own firsthand experiences. Instead, being afraid of wolves comes from what we have heard about them from other people and sources. Once such an association is made, however, the claim that wolves are to be feared and avoided may be firmly fixed in our minds despite the lack of any real evidence in support of it. What Gordon Allport wrote about the origins of prejudice may not have been the complete answer to the old question of why people are prejudiced, but he was not entirely wrong.

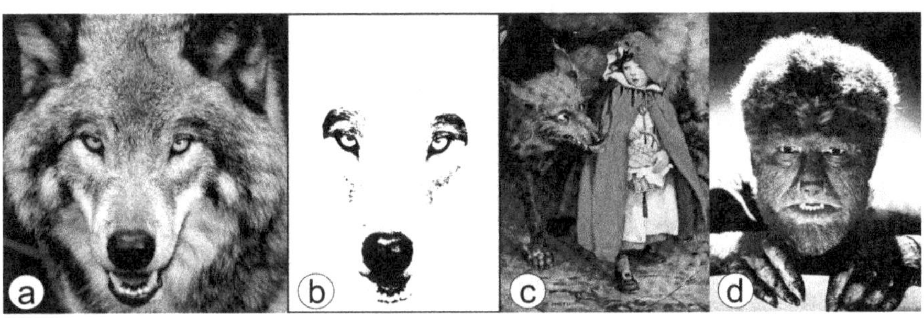

Figure 2.5. (a) A wolf (*Canis lupus*). Source: Steve, Pexel, Public Domain. (b) Visualization of a memory tracing of the distinctive patterning of this wolf's face. (c) "Little Red Riding Hood" (1911), an illustration for the European fairy tale about a small child and a crafty wolf. Source: Jessie Willcox Smith (1863–1935), Public domain, via Wikimedia Commons. (d) Magazine illustration of the actor Lon Chaney Jr. in makeup as "The Wolf Man" in the 1941 American horror movie from Universal Pictures. Source: Public domain, via Wikimedia Commons. © John Edward Terrell

Confronting Reality

Writing almost fifty years ago about how science is done, the Nobel Laureate François Jacob argued that regardless how mythic or scientific, the view of the world we have in our heads "is always largely a product of imagination." In keeping, however, with traditional Western scholarship since the Enlightenment hundreds of years ago, he then added this qualification: "For scientific thought, . . . imagination is only a part of the game. At every step, it has to meet with experimentation and criticism. . . . Science attempts to confront the possible with the actual" (1977: 1161).

Seeking after what is conventionally called the "truth" (also known as the "actual") is laudable. Yet this effort assumes we all have mental powers arguably beyond our reach even as *Homo sapiens*. Yes, as Jacob went on to say, science works by looking "for partial and provisional answers about those phenomena that can be isolated and well defined." Fair enough, and good luck doing this. However, what is all too easily overlooked from Jacob's point of view is that most of us are not scientists. We do not necessarily have the time and resources even to pretend we are.

Why Aren't We All Scientists?

There is a reason why doing science isn't for all of us. As large as it is, the human brain can do only some things well, other things only poorly, and some things not at all. And, yes, when this is acknowledged, what gets called prejudice can be seen less as a form of ignorance, and more as a side-effect of our innate limitations as living, breathing earthly creatures.

What is some of the evidence for saying this? It is obvious, for example, that our offspring take many years to grow up and become functioning adults. It is less obvious that one reason growing up for us takes so long is that our brains make astonishingly high-energy demands. It has been documented, for example, that "the brain's metabolic requirements peak in childhood, when it uses glucose at a rate equivalent to 66% of the body's resting metabolism and 43% of the body's daily energy requirement" (Kuzawa et al. 2014: 13010). The conclusion seems inescapable, although not altogether obvious, that the cost of brain development during childhood limits how fast body growth leading to adulthood can also happen.

Even when we are adults, however, having a brain to work with is costly. As an adult, your brain accounts for only about 2 percent of your body weight. It uses, however, about 20 percent of the energy consumed by your body at rest, making it third after skeletal muscle and the liver as the most energy-expensive components of the human body (Fonseca-Azevedo and Herculano-Houzel 2012; Mergenthaler et al. 2013).

Given how costly it is to run, "use your brain wisely" is more than just an old expression. As Mark van Rossum (2023) at the University of Nottingham has concluded, "the brain has likely evolved to be able to learn using as little energy as possible."

The "Truth Test"

Given how metabolically expensive it is to run a brain, it is not surprising that despite the popular notion that memories, like photographs, vividly capture all that you have experienced in life, in reality our memories are generally only as detailed and "true to life" as they need to be to see us through from day to day (Eagleman 2011: 27–30, 54; Eagleman 2015: 56; Seger and Miller 2010). Consequently, rather than thinking our memories are like photographic images or high-fidelity recordings, they are actually more like artistic impressions than faithful reproductions of what is "really out there" in the world beyond our bony skulls.

Therefore, as magnificent as it is, the human brain is predisposed to accept without too much bother that if something looks like a duck, swims like a duck, and quacks like a duck, then it probably is a duck. Said more formally, if something comes across to us as seemingly the same as something we have already experienced, we are predisposed to believe "this is just that again" despite the fact that in reality it may not be "just another one of those" (Figure 2.6, left). Often such pragmatic "similarity thinking" is good enough, and yet such seemingly lazy thinking can also make it easy for us to make mistakes and miss the fact that something really is not the same kind of thing or event we have experienced before.

Although not as widely recognized as this famous "Duck Test," there is a similar test often used that we call the "Truth Test." *If you trust the source, it sounds possible, and fits your beliefs, then it is true.*

There is no denying that both of these tests are about how easily such *categorical thinking* can be an efficient and practical way of dealing with life and everyday events (Allport 1954: 170–72, 175–76; Tversky and Kahneman 1974). We live in a world, however, that is *relational*, not categorical. Despite what common sense may tell us, things do not exist first and foremost all on their own, and then only later become connected with, linked to, tied to, and dependent on other similarly "disconnected" things. More often than not, things are the way they are because they are connected with and linked to other things.

It is an old truism to say that "the whole is more than the sum of its parts." This claim underplays that the character of what are seen as "parts" often depends on what else they are "part of." The chicken in a soup is decidedly different from the chicken pecking its way around in a barnyard (Figure 2.6, right). Labeling this ingredient in the soup as the "same" ignores how different the chicken has become by being defeathered, skinned, and cut up into nice bite-size pieces.

Understanding Prejudice

Here then is the basic premise of this book. To understand prejudice and why we are all capable of being prejudiced, you need to step back and see what we humans are capable of doing in the larger perspective of how our brains work, and what it takes for each of us to make it through life

Figure 2.6. The *categorical* "either/or" thinking needed to select the ducks shown in the CAPTCHA test on the left is fundamentally different from the *relational* thinking illustrated here using a recipe for homemade chicken soup. CAPTCHA = *Completely Automated Public Turing test to tell Computers and Humans Apart*. Ducks imagery: Pranavspn, CC BY-SA 3.0, via Wikimedia Commons. © John Edward Terrell

reasonably safe and sound. The conventional argument that prejudice is largely a consequence of ignorance brought about by geographic and/or social isolation is not entirely wrong. Yet this view misses too much about how we all deal with the world around us.

What needs to be weighed along with isolation and the need, or desire, to see the world be the way we want it to be are the *practical limitations* of the human brain as a biologically constructed thinking machine. Prejudice, pure and simple, is an example of what can be called categorical thinking. Although some have described this way of thinking as "quick and dirty," "heuristic," and even "lazy" (Kahneman 2011; Terrell et al. 2025: 3), from a biological point of view this type of thinking is metabolically "cost effective." Consequently, categorical thinking can also be described as *default thinking*—as an easy way of dealing with life that may not be perfect, but is generally good enough to see us through from day to day (Gordon Allport would agree; see Allport 1954: 24, 27).

It takes more work, and definitely more metabolic energy, to be more actively aware of what is happening around us—to see people, things, and events as "more or less" rather than simply as A or B, either/or, this or that (Giménez-Fernández et al. 2020). It is even harder and a lot more metabolically costly to track what is happening around us closely enough to grasp not just *what* is actually going on but also *why*.

In this chapter, we have tried to frame and model how easy it is to reach conclusions about people, things, and events that may seem "good enough," but that can be not only prejudiced but also harmful. In the following chapter, we survey the nature of prejudice in three places on earth that are half a world away from one another. These three examples show that *what* people can be prejudiced about can be astonishingly unpredictable. *Why* they are prejudiced, nevertheless, is often far less difficult to understand.

Key Points

1. It is easy to overlook that all of us are not as clever as we may want to believe we are. When this is acknowledged, what gets called prejudice can be seen less as a form of ignorance, and more as a side-effect of our innate limitations as living creatures.
2. To understand prejudice and why we are all capable of being prejudiced, we need to step back and see what we are capable of doing in the larger perspective of how our brains work, and what it takes for each of us to make it through life reasonably safe and sound.
3. Prejudice is an example of *categorical thinking*. Although some have described this way of thinking as "quick and dirty," "heuristic," and even

"lazy," from a biological point of view this type of thinking is metabolically "cost effective."

4. Therefore, categorical thinking can also be described as *default thinking*—as an easy way of dealing with life that may not be perfect, but is generally good enough to see us through from day to day.

3

Three Case Studies

The case studies discussed in this chapter may be about places on earth that are seemingly worlds apart, but they illustrate what we have come to think of as the "three Cs of prejudice." Despite the still popular claim that prejudice is basically a consequence of simple ignorance and social persuasion, our prejudices are ample evidence of how human it is to rely on *categorization* when we are trying to negotiate the otherwise overwhelming complexities of the real world. These case studies also show how *contingent*, varying, and changeable the characteristics, assumptions, and beliefs are that collectively comprise the signs and substance of prejudice at work in our lives. They document, too, how far we are prepared to go as human beings to maintain mastery and *control* over our "lives, fortunes, and sacred honor."

These are words enshrined at the very end of the Declaration of Independence unanimously adopted on July 4, 1776. This foundational document was signed by the fifty-six delegates representing the thirteen original states of the United States at the Second Continental Congress. It may not be conventional to see this declaration as a classic example of prejudice, but however much we agree with what is said so forcefully therein, this document is a fine example of the role of prejudice not only in our daily lives but in global politics, as well.

A Sea of Prejudice in the Latin American Melting Pot

You work day and night in the fields of the Caribbean island of St. Thomas to bring food to the table for you and your family. You hear about a mythical place called Panama, a land where the streets are paved with gold. Work-hungry, and literally hungry, you decide it is time to

> leave the island and try your fortune. You cannot pass the opportunity to earn three times your usual daily rate as a plantation laborer in your native Jamaica.
>
> Your mother cries, your siblings complain, but you keep at it. It's an easy decision in many ways: Life on St. Thomas is harder than usual, never mind that slavery ended a few decades ago. The people building the Panama Canal don't even ask you for a passport, let alone a visa. If you cannot afford to save for a ship ticket, the Canal recruiter will pay for it. And if things don't work as planned, you can always return. These days, you can even choose between a British or an American steamship line since there is more than one ship sailing to Panama's port city of Colón every single day. Who knows, you might become one of those men your father admires so much and who comes to visit on the holidays with elegant clothes and gifts for everyone. A man of means and worldly, a Colón man.

It must have been a scene to remember for people throughout the Antilles to view ships docked, waiting for able men (and some women) to travel to the Central American country of Panama for assumed temporary work in the late nineteenth century. Crowds of Afro-Antillean men lined up in Caribbean docks to try their luck. Going to Panama was "the greatest event of its time, imprinting itself on the consciousness of a generation" of islands starting in the mid-nineteenth century (Senior 2014: 9).

The Central American country of Panama is one of the most ethnically diverse countries in the Americas due to its geopolitical position as a "place of transit" and commerce crossroads. Resulting from important infrastructural projects—the Panamanian railroad (1850–55); the French (1881–90) and U.S. (1904–14) efforts to build the Panama Canal, and the construction of the Canal's third locks (1940–42)—thousands of workers from the Caribbean, South America, Europe, and Asia settled temporarily or permanently in the country, producing a "melting pot" like no other. But people of African descent from the Antilles came in more significant numbers than any other group. During this time, Panama experienced, in the words of historian George Reid Andrews (2004), a "blackening period."

Today, eight Indigenous groups and at least two distinct Afro-Panamanian groups, Asian Panamanians, rural and urban mestizo groups, and increasingly large numbers of resident expatriates inhabit the country's 29,157 square miles. In practical terms, Panama's racial and ethnic diversity is undeniable. But personal, social, and institutional prejudice has also accompanied this diversity. This apparent contradiction brings to the forefront the following question: How is prejudice lived in a self-proclaimed racial democracy?

Panama, the "Latin American Melting Pot"

Many Panamanians are proud of the country's label of being a "racial democracy." The label is connected to a myth of egalitarianism that has persisted in constructing this young nation-state. Egalitarianism presumes that, in addition to legal avenues that support the rights of people of all social races and groups, the way people think about and understand other groups who are part of this territory is positive (Guerrón Montero 2020).

How can we reconcile, then, this deeply ingrained idea of egalitarianism with the constant recognition of differences and the pervasive presence of racial inequality? How to explain the prevalence of the "melting pot" metaphor in Panama's ethos? One answer can be found in this country's history, tightly connected to its condition as a trade zone and "place of transit" since colonial times. After independence from Spain in 1821, and in contrast with most Latin American countries, Panama voluntarily annexed itself to the Gran Colombia (which included Ecuador, Venezuela, Peru, and Bolivia) in 1822. In 1830, Panama became part of Colombia. In 1903, it declared its independence from this country and became its own nation-state, only to become a de facto protectorate of the United States.

These historical facts are important because, in one version of the story of prejudice in Panama, both prejudice and racism do not characterize the Panamanian essence naturally because this country's geopolitical position as a place of transit has produced a long history of miscegenation. The commonly shared phrase "everyone is a Zulú" is used by many Panamanians to signal that they carry in them a complex ethnic mixture that negates any possibility of racial or ethnic prejudice (Guerrón Montero 2006). Thus, prejudice and racism are cast as ills brought about by the United States on Panamanian soil.

In fact, when the United States government started the construction of the Panama Canal in the early twentieth century, they brought with them the apartheid-like system commonly called Jim Crow. At the core of this system was the assumption that Blacks and Whites were fundamentally different kinds of human beings belonging to distinct, unequally positioned races (as discussed in Chapter 1). The system was transplanted to the ten-mile stretch known as the Panama Canal Zone, where workers were assigned to a "Golden Roll" and a "Silver Roll." These distinctions were exclusively based on skin color, regardless of place of origin or occupation, although non-American White workers needed to undergo a further filtration process before joining the Golden Roll.[1] Afro-Antillean and Mestizo Panamanians were confined to the Silver Roll and endured discriminatory practices that completely ignored the "essential dignity of human beings" (GWC, SCRBC, 63/10; Westerman 1950: 1). While this

Figure 3.1. Jamaican laborers building the Panama Canal for the Compagnie Universelle du Canal Interocéanique de Panama, circa 1885. Unknown photographer, National Museum of Science & Media/Science & Society Picture Library. Public domain via Wikimedia Commons.

racist legal framework was limited to the Canal Zone, the ideas that separated peoples based on color spread out around the country in the form of prejudice, if not as discriminatory laws.

Effectively, two racial systems coexisted in the Canal Zone: the binary racial system characteristic of the United States and the Panamanian multiracial mestizo system that produced Canal workers (Náder Durango 2020: 85). The former only recognized whiteness and blackness; the latter was composed of diverse ethnic groups, all struggling for political recognition, territorial rights, and anti-discriminatory legislation. In both cases, non-White workers were met with exclusion, prejudice, and racism (Sigler et al. 2014). The Jim Crow system in the Canal Zone contributed to the narrative that any kind of prejudice, segregation, or racism present in the country resulted from the U.S. presence or from U.S. influence. Panamanians did not have prejudices; the Americans did. Panamanians did not divide the country into two (natives and Americans); the Americans did. The story becomes more complicated because of the added assumption that Panamanians favored a democratic stance toward racial relations in contrast with the U.S. Thus, favoring a melting pot represented a *nationalist* stance against United States intervention.

But this is only one part of the story. Panama experienced segregation long before the establishment of the Panama Canal. By the mid-nineteenth century, social Darwinism was alive and thriving among Panamanian elites, who looked at European powers for guidance and inspiration. These elites attributed the marginalization they experienced at the hands of the Colombian authorities to the visible, undeniable presence of Indigenous peoples and peoples of African descent in their territory (Náder Durango 2020: 79).

It followed that Panama's "real essence" was to be found in its central provinces (Herrera, Los Santos, Coclé, and Veraguas), colonized primarily by peoples of Spanish descent (Jurado 1978). These provinces were not "tainted" by the racial and ethnic diversity found in the cities of Panama City and Colón or in the forgotten western province of Bocas del Toro. The presence of peoples of African descent from the Caribbean or Americans of all ethnicities was "a danger to the real identity, which can no longer be found in the cities, where those exotic masses are heaped up" (Ibáñez Castejón 2021: 24). Here, the United States' lingering influence was also felt, as the first attempts to create a unified identity were made *in response* to the physical and cultural presence of the United States in Panama. To disassociate from neocolonial structures, signal independence, and establish an identity in synch with Latin American roots, Panamanians stressed their Hispanic origins, thus erasing blackness from their history.

A Certain Tropical Style of Racial Democracy

> You work day and night in the fields of La Pintada in Coclé to bring food to the table for you and your family. There never seem to be enough hours of the day to clear the dry, dense forests to make way for more fields and tend to them, and there never seems to be enough corn or rice during harvest despite all your efforts. You have heard that the situation is different in other parts of Panama: In the remote province of Bocas del Toro, banana plantations abound; people (the wrong kind of people) are becoming rich with the "Green Gold" boom. These people are foreigners, not even real Panamanians; they don't speak Spanish or know anything about this country. Why are they—with their different customs, food, language, and ideas—receiving more benefits than you, a real Panamanian, a poor peasant from the central provinces?

During the first half of the twentieth century, blackness became a synonym for an Antillean identity and for backwardness, and blackness was all that was wrong about Panama. Having a majority population of people with black skin greatly concerned government officials and members of the elite. The narratives that excluded Afro-Antilleans from the technical advances and the economic boom that resulted from the Panama Canal construction presented them as "anti-national aberrations that oppressed the local workers by inundating the market with cheap labor force" (Lasso 2013: 51). Ironically, Afro-Antilleans were at the center of both these technical advances and economic boom. They were the architects of the development of capitalism in Panama and the "progress" that ensued, as they participated in different capacities in the crucial infrastructural projects that placed Panama on the map.

Yet prejudices against Afro-Antilleans came from all sides. We have defined prejudice in this book as a way of thinking and behaving, as something we do. We have also proposed that there are at least three kinds of prejudices: personal, social, and institutional. In the Latin American "melting pot," these prejudices were experienced in relation to blackness and some of the cultural practices attributed to being Afro-Antillean (Guerrón Montero 2012). Take hair, for example. Hair, and more specifically, hair texture, was and is a way to establish both beauty and identity; personal prejudices toward blackness are translated into daily efforts by many Panamanian men and women—including Afro-Antilleans—to straighten their so-called *pelo malo* (bad hair) using pomades and brassy chemical treatments. Identifying woolen hair in others (grouping or classification), labeling woolen hair in others and oneself (grading or evaluation) as unsuitable, and taking steps to "tame it" illustrates the reach of personal prejudice.

At the social level, the inscription of prejudices about peoples of African descent in their own bodies spearheaded the very process that brought large numbers of Afro-Antilleans to Panama. As we discussed in Chapter 1, during the nineteenth century, according to social Darwinist and climatological understandings of racial relations, Blacks and Whites were believed to be fundamentally different. Peoples of African descent were thought to be immune to tropical diseases such as malaria and yellow fever and inherently adapted to hard labor. This belief was shared throughout the Americas, helping legitimize African slavery and slaveholding and shaping the strategies used by Britain and France in defending their Caribbean colonies in the nineteenth century. It was also extended to Indigenous peoples in territories occupied by the British, even for short periods, such as the Philippines.[2] Native workers' health was neglected, so they were not treated when ill. This situation generated a self-fulfilled prophecy and the "pervasive arguments that these subject populations had innate immunities to the diseases that were so harmful to the newly arrived colonial forces. Whether considering dysentery, smallpox, typhoid,

Figure 3.2. Advertisement for Sweet Georgia Brown Hair Pomade in *The Panama Tribune* on Sunday, December 2, 1945 (No. 881, page 8). *The Panama Tribune* was an English-language weekly newspaper established in Panama in 1928 and considered the voice of Afro-Antilleans in the country [Schomburg Center for Research in Black Culture].

or malaria, colonial doctors viewed whites as particularly vulnerable" (Espinosa 2014: 448).

In Panama, this belief made Afro-Antillean workers the ideal labor force to participate in infrastructural projects in the tropics. Thus, the efforts of William Crawford Gorgas, the U.S. Army sanitarian who oversaw the elimination of yellow fever from the Panama Canal Zone during its construction, were focused on making the region safe for "the White man" because "the Black man" was believed to be already naturally equipped to resist tropical diseases (Espinosa 2014: 437). While not all scholars agree on this perspective, and many believed that frequent exposure to the diseases was what created more resistance, the first assumption prevailed.

At the institutional level, numerous laws were passed during the twentieth century to prevent the further "blackening" of Panama. For example, Article 17 of Law No. 54 of 1938 established that persons of "prohibited" immigration needed to deposit five hundred U.S. dollars to enter the country for a maximum of thirty days. Those individuals in the "prohibited" category included "English-speaking Negroes, Chinese, Armenians, Arabs, Turks, Hindus, Syrians, Lebanese, Palestinians and North Africans of the Turkish race" (GWC, SCRBC, 63/9; Villiers 1963: 1-2).[3] This situation became even more palpable when Dr. Arnulfo Arias Madrid (1901–1988) came to power. Arias Madrid was a Panamanian politician, medical doctor, and writer who served as the president of Panama three times for varying periods (1940–41, 1949–51, and 1968). Arias Madrid was a Harvard- and University of Chicago-educated medical doctor and surgeon specializing in psychiatry, obstetrics, and endocrinology. He modeled himself after Italian dictator Benito Mussolini and sanctioned racial and ethnic discrimination through the Constitution of 1941. This Constitution legally excluded Afro-Antilleans, Chinese, Syrians, and Turks from becoming Panamanian citizens or migrating to Panama (Arango 1999: 14–20; *Panama Tribune* 1940: 1). This legal discrimination was justified through sociocultural and economic arguments. While the Constitution was suspended in 1945 and replaced by a new constitution in 1946, the damage was done.

Even Afro-Antillean tourists, especially those whose first language was English, did not escape from these discriminatory practices against "Negroes who wish to enter the country," despite laws implemented to counter previous policies. For example, in July 1953, the Consul General of Panama in New York issued a fifteen-day permit to six white delegates to the 7th International Conference of the international relief organization CARE held in Panama City and a three-day permit to two African American delegates (GWC, SCRBC, 63/9; Villiers 1963: 1-2). When this discriminatory application of the laws was brought to the attention of then-president José Antonio Remón Cantera (1952–55), he stated, "I am head of a government which does not harbor racial prejudices of any kind neither in thought nor in action. . . . We are all equal before God and before the law" (GWC, SCRBC, 63/9; Villiers 1963: 3; see also Westerman n.d.).

Nonetheless, these practices prevailed. Law No. 16 (June 30, 1960) established that all visitors from friendly nations could freely travel to Panama without needing a visa. Yet, Afro-Antilleans—particularly Jamaicans—were required to apply for a visa to the Ministry of Foreign Relations to visit Panama as tourists (GWC, SCRBC, 63/9; Villiers 1963: 2). More than one commentator pointed out not only the absurd and unjust behavior evidenced in these policies, but also its inconsistency with Panama's firm condemnation of U.S. discrimination in the Canal Zone (GWC, SCRBC, 64/1; *La Estrella* and *El Día*, April 29, 1963). Afro-Antillean intellectuals such as the self-made scholar and journalist George Westerman put up a "one-man fight" throughout the years to shine a light on these discriminatory practices to Panamanian authorities and "to purge Panama's immigration system of its prejudicial practices" (GWC, SCRBC, 63/9, 64/1; Villiers 1963: 2). In an editorial note for *The Panama Tribune* written in 1949, Westerman summarized the contributions of Afro-Antilleans to Panama as follows:

> The West Indian [Afro-Antillean] came to the Isthmus 98 years ago as a wage earner in industries and as such he has remained, except in a few isolated cases. He has not been the trader to scrape wealth and send it away. Because of his original training and his natural bent, coupled with the fact that his language or dialect—the predominant English—is the language of the chief industries in the Republic, he has always been the backbone of the industrial life of the Isthmian community. So with brawn and brain he has helped to transform Panama from a pesthole of diseases and a land of swamps and jungles, into its present condition of advanced sanitation (Westerman 1949).

Today, the belief that Afro-Antilleans are Panamanians "only by convenience" and "have not adopted our customs, idiosyncrasies, etc." remains (*Panama Tribune* 1958: 1).

Conclusions

The following conversation is a composite of numerous interviews conducted by one of the authors of this book over more than two decades of ethnographic research in Panama, followed by an intervention from Afro-Antillean poet and novelist Carlos Guillermo Wilson, alias Cubena. This short conversation captures the views of many Panamanians and illustrates the universal nature of prejudice; some of the stereotypes mentioned in the dialogue could refer to various cultures and not just Panamanian Afro-Antilleans.

> Interviewer: I want to understand why you think a person from the British West Indies would be inferior to you. What are the characteristics of Afro-Antilleans that you find different from yours?
>
> Any Panamanian: I am not a racist, but *Chombos* [defined below] are the worst. I am sorry to tell you this, but it is true. They are filthy because they eat a lot of curry and fish; they have strange beliefs. They speak strangely; they rarely learn Spanish because they prefer their broken English or patois, and when they are forced to speak Spanish, they have this thick accent that betrays them. They are strange; they are not like us.
>
> People tell *me* I speak Spanish as a Panamanian: I call everyone *tu* [an informal "you"], I change English words to fit into Spanish, I "eat" letter sounds when I speak, and the *rabiblancos* [elite Panamanians] call me uneducated. But compared to the Chombos and their broken way of speaking English and Spanish, my speech is perfect!
>
> Interviewer: I am not familiar with the term *Chombo*. Could you explain it to me?
>
> Any Panamanian: Here in Panama, we use the word *Chombo* for Black people born in Jamaica, Barbados, Martinique, St. Vincent, etc., or descended from them. Those people are different from the people who came as slaves to Panama, learned to speak Spanish, and became Catholic. The Chombos are so different from anyone else that we have a saying here in Panama: The Chombo is a Chombo. It's about being Black, but it's more than that; it's about speaking broken English and patois, but it's also more than that. It's about the habits and practices that separate them from us, the rest of the Panamanians.
>
> Cubena: Many Panamanians hate the Chombos because they are not all Catholics (since their grandparents were originally from the West Indies, many of them practice other religions); because they prefer to speak French and English in their homes, and finally because, according to racist Panamanians, too many Chombos have failed to participate sufficiently in the process of ethnic whitening in order to "better the race"—or to put it more frankly, to erase all that is African. As a result, all traces of an African gene or phenotype are hated and rejected: the woolen hair, the flat, broad nose, the thick lips, and above all, the black skin of the Chombos. (Wilson 1998: 41)

The phrase "I am not a racist, but *Chombos* are the worst" illustrates the difficulties that people have associating prejudice with positive thoughts. According to social psychologist Michael Billig, the prototype of prejudice is "not any opinion formed without judgment, but nationalist, or racist, opinions in particular" (2012: 145). In his words, the use of the phrase "I am not a racist, but" or "I am not prejudiced, but" is not simply a defense of rational thought "but is a defense against that particular sort of irrationality that leads to hostility against individuals based upon the color of their skin or the provenance of their passport" (145).

The neocolonial intervention and discriminatory laws implemented by the United States in the Canal Zone were palpable and had grave consequences still experienced today throughout Panama. However, they were also used as excuses to free Panama from the responsibility of confronting its own prejudices. Like a cobweb, personal, social, and institutional prejudices are entangled in how Panamanians view themselves and others and behave toward themselves and others today.

The Contingent Nature of Prejudice in the Eastern Highlands of Papua New Guinea

> Police are warning a "all-out war" could erupt in Eastern Highlands province in Papua New Guinea, after 19 people were killed in tribal violence late last week. High-powered weapons, as well as a hand grenade, were used in fighting on Thursday and Friday near Kainantu Town in the east of the country, causing 19 deaths, with many more people unaccounted for, and properties destroyed. The fighting, between the Agarabi and Tapo clans, was over a land ownership dispute and broke out just miles outside from Kainantu Town in Eastern Highlands Province. . . . "A lot of reports coming in that tomorrow will be an all-out war between the two factions as they have by now amassed arms over the weekend," Provincial Police Commander Michael Welly wrote in his report. . . . "Last week Thursday, both parties from the Agarabi and the Tapo tribe came into town to sign that peace settlement agreement, however, tension was very high at that time and when a fight broke out between two women over a domestic issue, it just triggered the full battle as one party thought they were being attacked and the other party thought the same." (Kuku 2021)

With more than eight hundred languages, Papua New Guinea (PNG) is the most linguistically diverse country in the world. As we saw in the previous case study, language differences, often also understood as ethnic differences, can indeed be one of the things people can be very prejudiced about. This news article by Papua New Guinean journalist Rebecca Kuku in the British newspaper *The Guardian*, in contrast, reports of an armed conflict between people from two named entities, Tapo and Agarabi, that speak the same language (also called Agarabi), live in close neighborhood to each other, and who to an outsider might be impossible to distinguish. Despite their cultural similarities, people from both sides assumed that the other side was ready to resort to violence at the slightest provocation. So much so that a conflict over land that at first seemed settled through mediation and a peace agreement completely spiraled out of control and developed into this "all-out war," which went on for three weeks and in the end cost twenty-three people their lives and led to the destruction and burning of dozens of houses and businesses. But what kind of entities are Tapo and Agarabi, and why were they variously called clan, faction, or tribe? And what does this particular case of "all-out war" have to do with prejudice?

The Eastern Highlands of Papua New Guinea is a close-knit world of rural villages, home to hard-working people primarily engaged in subsistence farming and small-scale coffee production. While the people in these communities are often enough peaceful and friendly, they are also always seemingly teetering on the brink of "all-out war." In this case study, we will explore the role of intergroup distrust, and particularly sorcery accusations as expressions of prejudice, as constitutive elements for intergroup conflict. Looking at both precolonial and postcolonial dynamics of group formation and warfare, we will show how prejudice in the Eastern Highlands of PNG is distinct from previous examples in that it is based on different conceptions of difference between people. At the same time, prejudice is constantly changing and adapting to shifting political situations, and not as fixed and permanent as one often might be led to believe. Neither are the groups involved in these conflicts.

Finding Groups in the Highlands of New Guinea

As we have mentioned in the Introduction, we have concluded that groups as such do not exist, in the sense that they cannot be seen as a sort of collective actor with their own ideas, motives, or interests. What does exist, however, are people who live together, work together, claim and defend a common territory—in other words, form a community—and see themselves as separate from other people who live nearby. Anthropologists usually call these communities "local groups" but argue about their definition and how they are composed. In New Guinea in particular, anthropologists came to realize that these local groups are not nearly as neatly bounded and permanent as they first thought.

The central spine of the island of New Guinea, the second-largest island of the world, was once considered to be sparsely inhabited at best, if at all. From the coast, the looming mountain ranges seemed too steep, too cragged, to support a large population. But when the first European gold prospectors, missionaries, and Australian colonial officers ventured into these mountains in the 1920s and 1930s, they found nestled within them wide, fertile valleys supporting hundreds of thousands of people living in thousands of communities. These communities in the Eastern Highlands were relatively small, on average around a hundred fifty to two hundred fifty people, and each local group was economically mostly self-sufficient, politically independent, enmeshed in often-changing relations of enmity and alliance with other groups, and engaged in frequent warfare.

When anthropologists first started to study these communities in the Highlands of New Guinea in the late 1940s and 1950s, they did so equipped with theoretical ideas about group composition derived from previous anthropological research done in Africa. These models emphasized agnatic (male-line) descent as the primary basis for memberships in social groups called patrilineal tribes. A typical social group was thus seen as consisting of related males, who all can claim descent from a common ancestor. But the reality in the New Guinea Highlands did not fit these theoretical models. Local groups still served as the primary social, political, and economic units, typically defined by shared residence, defense of a common territory, and mutual cooperation. And the people in those local groups sure enough spoke of themselves as related, emphasizing that the solidarity of all group members was based on kinship (Schwörer 2020: 34–38). But while genealogical connections were symbolically emphasized, anthropological studies revealed that many local groups included a significant proportion of males who were not agnatically related, sometimes up to 30 percent (Robbins 1982: 119). The people appeared to be quite flexible and inclusive, readily accepting nonkin members as part of their local groups rather than being keen on excluding them. This openness to incorporating newcomers was often due to the necessity of maintaining group strength during times of warfare when each able-bodied man was considered an additional military asset.

Within local groups, kinship units such as extended families or lineages as well as clans provided a framework for rituals, alliances, common decision-making, and conflict resolution. Lineages consisted of individuals tracing descent to a known ancestor, though genealogical knowledge was shallow and varied depending on individual perspectives and political needs. Clans, larger than lineages, were named exogamous units, meaning that one could only marry women from a different clan. Members of the same clan claimed descent from a common, though often mythical, ancestor. Usually, there were several clans within one local group, and members of the same clan might live in different local groups and would not necessarily share the same interests. In some cases, multiple clans were considered to belong to the same phratry or tribe, the largest genealogically defined units (Schwörer 2020: 34–38). But all those units were less significant in daily life than the territorially defined local groups, like Tapo and Agarabi in the opening quote, which are thus neither clans nor tribes.

Membership in local groups often depended on multiple factors, including residence, shared resources, participation in communal activities (e.g., feasting, house building, or exchange), and reciprocal relationships, rather than strictly on genealogical ties. Kinship itself was often defined less by biological descent and more by co-residence and the nurturing, cooperative behaviors exhibited among group members. The anthropologist L. L. Langness noted that "the simple fact of residence in a Korofeigu group can and does determine kinship. People do not, necessarily, reside where they do because they are kinsmen, rather, they become kinsmen because they reside there" (1964: 50). Indeed, reciprocal and cooperative behaviors defined kin-like ties, allowing individuals to forge meaningful connections with affines (in-laws), friends, agemates, and even trading partners in other villages. These relationships were critical for political ambitions and survival, particularly during times of instability and warfare. Refugees fleeing from wars elsewhere would be readily incorporated into local groups. In fact, individuals often moved between local groups, where they were quickly integrated if they had preexisting social ties or demonstrated reciprocal behavior (Watson 1983: 9–10). Kinship, therefore, was not a fixed system but one that was adaptable and responsive to changing circumstances.

The dynamic nature of Highland societies was further shaped by endemic warfare, which drove frequent processes of fission and fusion. Local groups often split when populations grew too large, or when conflicts developed between factions within a group, leading to the formation of new groups. Members of the newly established group might still maintain close ties to their parent groups if the split was amicable. They might in fact move back and forth, being welcomed as members of both groups. Conversely, people from two or more groups (or factions thereof) might fuse when circumstances required stronger collective defense or cooperation. But local groups might also completely dissolve, particularly after military defeats, when members of the defeated group were chased off their territory by the victorious party. In these cases, surviving members of the local group sought refuge in different neighboring groups with which they were on friendly terms, and where some of their kin or affines were already living. When circumstances changed, they might reunite and reclaim their old territory, but that was never guaranteed (Watson 1983: 242–47; Berndt 1971: 387–88, 410–11). Such changes in group composition were frequent, reflecting the constant flux in social and territorial arrangements.

Local Identity and the Roots of Prejudice

With the impermanence of local groups, the fact that people are constantly interacting with members of neighboring groups, and the added difficulty of finding distinctions between adjoining communities even when they would be speaking different languages, one would assume limited chances for prejudice to develop. But in the 1960s, ethnographer James B. Watson found out that there was a tendency to see other communities as completely different people: "As an ethnographer working in Kainantu Subdistrict, I came to a paradoxical conclusion: no matter how numerous, small, near, and nearly identical the polities of the Eastern Highlands may be, no matter how permeable their boundaries or how checkered the history of their membership, they will consider themselves and will be thought to be distinct ethnic units" (1990: 18).

Watson at the time was leading a large-scale research project that intended to look at the evolution of cultural difference between the different linguistic groups in the Kainantu area of the Eastern Highlands. There were about forty to sixty thousand people living in the area at the time, speaking six larger and a number of smaller languages, in about a hundred fifty or so small communities. All these people were culturally similar; they were subsistence farmers growing sweet potatoes and taro, and raising pigs, and until the advent of the colonial administration they were involved in near-constant warfare. As part of the project, Watson and his wife, Virginia, interviewed people in one community about in- and out-group perception for a cross-cultural study on ethnocentrism that was administered to people all over the world. The very elaborate *Ethnocentrism Field Manual* they used to interview people about neighboring peoples that they considered as "outgroups" only had space for about four to five different entries, clearly anticipating that people would name large and encompassing ethnic or linguistic groups (Watson 1990: 19–20). But with the criteria given by the study, the people of one community of Tairora-speakers could enumerate easily over forty to sixty different outgroups that they considered different from themselves, and for each they could describe certain traits or stereotypes. Indeed, each neighboring community was considered different, but the further distant local groups were located, the more they were conflated into named larger groups, be it phratries or even linguistic groups (1990: 27).

To an outsider, thus, Kainantu people might look thoroughly homogeneous. But members of one local group take for granted that there are always a number of locally significant differences that distinguish them from the members of other groups. Among these differences were certain skills or powers, especially in manufacturing arrows, pottery, and in magic and sorcery, but also particular resources, local landscape features and distinctive artifacts, as well as stories, beliefs and traditions (1990: 23–26). It becomes clear, then, that as much as people in the Eastern Highlands might be similar, they will always find ample ground and ample reason to see themselves as separate and different from other people living in a neighboring community. And it is indeed among neighboring communities, between those with the most contact and with whom one has intermarried, allied, and fought wars, where differences are felt most strongly. There is an unstated assumption that people living elsewhere are automatically different, regardless of whether one is aware of any differences.

The reason for such difference is seen in the close connection of people to the environment in which they were brought up and continue to live. One of the most distinct differences is the one between people living in the grasslands, and those who live at the edge of the forests. While not innate, the ability to navigate and utilize the forest, for example, is deeply ingrained through upbringing and community influence rather than being purely genetic or acquired through formal instruction. This competence encompasses not only technical knowledge, like for example handling or cooking a python that lives in the forest, but also a profound familiarity with the magical powers of the land. Outsiders, such as grassland inhabitants, lack this deeply rooted connection and face inherent risks in attempting such tasks. The transmission of a local identity occurs through living within a specific community, partaking in its practices, and being shaped by its cultural and environmental context. Local waters, foods, and soils contribute to this process, as they carry unique efficacies—described as magical—that naturalize those who grow up consuming them. These elements, deeply tied to the land, form a reciprocal relationship whereby the land shapes its people, and the people, in turn, leave their imprint on the land (Watson 1990: 32–35).

The Eastern Highlands perspective on human development thus diverges sharply from certain Western notions stressing genetic determinism. Children are seen as clean slates when they are born, as malleable beings shaped by their environment and the collective efforts of their community. Through rituals, training, and active engagement, intangible qualities such as wisdom, competence, and immunity to the dangers of the environment are cultivated. This contrasts with more biological ideas that emphasize innate potential or preprogrammed destinies. Physical growth and individual achievements are seen by the people of the Eastern Highlands as products of effort and nurture, rather than predetermined inheritance. Their worldview emphasizes the interplay between the tangible and the intangible, between the physical environment and the magical or spiritual forces that permeate it, as the cornerstone of individual and communal identity (Watson 1990: 35–39). This worldview then also means that the basis for identity, and with it the basis for ideas about others, and therefore prejudices, are fundamentally different from our own.

Sorcery Accusations and Intergroup Warfare

In precolonial times, before the 1930s, all these local groups were deeply involved in a dynamic and shifting network of alliances, rivalries, and warfare. Conflicts were frequent, often occurring annually, and were driven by grievances such as theft, abduction, or accusations of sorcery, but also—and that is central for our book—by ideas and prejudices about other groups.

Warfare in the Eastern Highlands took two main forms: open-field battles and surprise raids. Open-field battles were more ritualized, with warriors forming loose lines to exchange arrows from a distance, typically resulting in minimal casualties due to the use of shields and evasive tactics. In contrast, surprise raids, often carried out at dawn, were stealthy and resulted in significantly higher casualties. Research by David Hayano on the Awa reveals that warfare accounted for approximately 30 percent of male deaths and 16 percent of female deaths, totaling 25 percent of all deaths over the fifty years before pacification (1974: 287). Similar findings were reported for the Usurufa, where 32 percent of men and 12 percent of women died due to armed conflict (Berndt 1971: 397–99). These figures are consistent with averages for war-related deaths in nonstate societies but are much higher than any casualty rates of states involved in modern warfare (when one compares war deaths in relation to the total population), underlining the considerable intensity of warfare in such communities.

This warfare was primarily motivated by revenge for perceived wrongs, rather than being initiated for strategic purposes. These grievances ensured a steady cycle of hostilities between local groups, as each act of violence often provoked further vengeance. Common causes for retaliation included disputes over marriage arrangements or the abduction or elopement of women, conflicts arising from the killing of or damage caused by runaway pigs, and deaths attributed to sorcery. Sorcery was regarded as a secretive method to harm or kill others, and in each local group there were typically a few men skilled in employing various techniques and supernatural means for such purposes. Severe illnesses and suspicious deaths—characterized by symptoms like weight loss, swelling, or sudden collapse—were frequently attributed to sorcery.

These sorcery practices were and still are widespread across the region, with some groups recognizing up to twenty distinct forms of sorcery. They can be categorized by the different techniques and implements people used and the mechanism of action they ascribed to each type of sorcery. One common form of sorcery is leavings sorcery, where bodily substances or personal items like hair, fingernails, or food scraps are bundled up with sorcery materials and treated in ways such as roasting or burying to harm the target. Another form involves poisoning, where magical (but often nontoxic) substances are applied to the skin of the victim, to arrows, or mixed with consumables like food and water. Projectile sorcery entails magically "shooting" harmful substances or objects into a victim's body, sometimes through hidden traps on paths or in homes that activate when approached. Soul assassination is also practiced, where a victim's soul is believed to be trapped in small animals like rats or lizards, which are then killed to harm the person. Additionally, assault sorcery involves physically attacking a person, rendering them unconscious, and performing invasive rituals such as inserting needles or supposedly removing internal organs, causing the victim to die within a specific timeframe (Schwörer 2017: 318).

Most deaths from illness, except for infants and the elderly or infirm, were blamed on enemy sorcery, prompting elaborate detection rituals to find out who was the sorcerer responsible for the death. Among the Fore, for example, possum livers were cooked in bamboo tubes and then examined, with undercooked livers signaling guilt. Similarly, the Auyana and Tairora used vegetables or sweet potatoes marked with suspects' names and cooked them; incomplete cooking or explosions of the bamboo cooking tubes indicated sorcery. Some rituals even involved the corpse, where physical reactions during ceremonies were interpreted as proof of sorcery (Schwörer 2020: 48). All these detection rituals have one thing in common: They rely on interpretation. Which is the sweet potato least cooked, for example. The assignment of guilt by these rituals was thus not random but shaped by existing prejudices about other groups, as well as social and geographic patterns.

Hayano (1973) notes for the Awa that the likelihood of sorcery accusations decreases with distance and is influenced by negative stereotypes and prejudices about neighboring groups. Such accusations were often directed at immediately neighboring groups, where interaction is most frequent and the potential for conflict is highest. And whenever there was conflict and tensions, people developed prejudices over time. Similarly, Lindenbaum (1979: 137–43) describes a "geography of fear" in the Highlands, where people in more densely populated central regions often viewed people living in sparsely settled peripheral areas as masters of sorcery. This pattern applies not only to regions but also to local groups. Fieldwork by Schwörer (2020) revealed that members of powerful local groups—those with greater numbers, military strength, cohesion, and economic success—tend to fear sorcery from less powerful groups with whom they have strained relations. Sorcery suspicions are often strategic, targeting weaker groups, as people living in such groups are seen as having to rely on sorcery as the only option to gain power or seek redress for perceived injustice, as they would not have the military might to settle their complaints on the battlefield.

Prejudices about other local groups, who are perceived as harboring potential sorcerers and blamed for causing the death of a group member, are thus contingent on the prevailing social relations between communities. A history of enmity or hostility with members of a particular local group, or perceptions of their weakness and inferiority, fosters stronger biases against them, making them more likely to be accused of causing suspicious deaths by sorcery compared to members of groups that are considered allies or equals. These lines of hostility and alliance, of inferiority and superiority or equality, have a habit of changing quickly, however. Former enemies may become allies within a few years, just as allies may become adversaries, inevitably altering the prejudices held against members of these same groups.

Changes Through Time

The precolonial warfare described previously was eventually curtailed by the Australian colonial administration, around Kainantu already in the mid-1930s, further away between the mid-1940s and the early 1960s. This process of pacification relied on the state's enforcement of a monopoly on violence through police actions and the implementation of a colonial justice system. Although some communities faced direct violence, such as arrests or corporal punishment, pacification often hinged on the psychological impact of such actions and the allure of Western goods controlled by colonial authorities. These goods, tied to hopes of wealth and peace, gained an outsized influence due to rapid societal change. In the long term, nonviolent strategies proved most effective. Colonial officers acted as mediators and judges, providing alternatives to violence, while Indigenous leaders helped enforce peace by integrating these new systems with traditional leadership structures. The resulting "peace dividend" of stability and prosperity disincentivized warfare, especially as pacification brought tangible benefits (Schwörer 2021).

With the cessation of warfare, people could now travel much more freely than before and encountered new people and new groups, which automatically meant that they also developed new prejudices. From the 1950s onward, many young men from all over the Highlands were hired as plantation laborers down on the coast or on the other islands of New Guinea. On these plantations, they were grouped and housed together with people from the same region, usually named for the government station where they were recruited. People from one Highlands region, who at home considered themselves to be different, now suddenly had to cooperate with each other, and with this cooperation they developed a shared identity to distinguish themselves from people from other regions of the Highlands, and people from the coastal or island regions. With the encounter of people who now not only sounded and behaved but also looked completely different, there was also a felt change in explanations for difference, away from the previous emphasis on notions of nurture and the environment, more toward ideas of inheritance. As Beer (2006) showed for a lowland group in Papua New Guinea, similar ideas of changeable cultural otherness as held in the Eastern Highlands were replaced within two generations by stereotypes of inherited and unchangeable bodily differences.

With the end of warfare and the freedom of movement, intergroup distrust and sorcery fears did not disappear, however, but continued to evolve. The newfound freedom of movement was also seen to facilitate the mobility of sorcerers, who were rumored to travel long distances to offer their services. Increased inter-ethnic contact led to the spread and evolution of sorcery techniques. New forms of sorcery emerged, often more potent than traditional types and lacking known countermeasures. And with open warfare prohibited by the administration, sorcery, as it was a secretive affair, was seen as an even more important outlet for intergroup hostility and as the primary form of retaliation that was still available for people holding grudges. But the impact of this process varied regionally. While sorcery deaths in the Awa village of Tauna, for example, did not increase (Hayano 1973: 187), neighboring Ilakia experienced a significant rise (Boyd 1996: 47). Among the Agarabi and northern Tairora, sorcery cases initially decreased after pacification but surged in the 1960s, surpassing precolonial levels, particularly during land disputes (Westermark 1981: 93–95).

What also changed was the direction from which sorcery was thought to emanate: Traditionally, sorcery was believed to originate from members of enemy local groups outside one's community, and accusations rarely occurred within hamlets, villages, or alliances. However, socioeconomic changes, such as increased competition over resources like land for coffee and cattle projects, have led to a shift toward endo-sorcery, where suspicion arises within formerly "safe" local groups. Westermark (1981, 1984) observed this transformation among the Agarabi in the 1970s, where jealousy and internal rivalry fueled accusations of sorcery within villages, destabilizing whole communities. And in the Awa village of Ilakia, such suspicions led to a significant decline in community cohesion, prompting residents to leave for other areas or seek coastal employment (Boyd 1996).

This contraction of "zones of safety," as Lindenbaum (1981: 119–120) describes them, reflects a broader cultural shift. The interaction of formerly egalitarian communities with market-based economic systems through trade and wage labor has created conflicts of values that exacerbate internal tensions. The social inequality that developed with the planting of coffee in particular created a lot of envy and jealousy, which are seen as the main motivating factors for sorcerers to attack and harm others. Rapid population growth further contributes to these changes, transforming once-intimate face-to-face communities into larger, fragmented entities. The Auyana local group of Amaira, for instance, grew from 245 people in 1953 to 745 by 2000, splitting into four distinct settlement clusters. During this time, sorcery accusations between the most distant clusters became frequent and culminated in an armed conflict in 2006.

After one or two generations living in peace, sporadic warfare between local groups had resurfaced in the Eastern Highlands during the late 1970s and early 1980s. Initially quickly curbed by police intervention, by the late 1980s and 1990s armed conflicts escalated unchecked, driven by the economic crises of that period, which undermined police effectiveness, overburdened the courts, and contributed to the declining reputation of both the police forces and the government as a whole. At the same time, wars that were once fought with bows and arrows have increasingly seen the use of homemade shotguns and, more recently, even assault rifles and hand grenades, leading to a dramatic rise in casualties.

Despite the example given at the beginning, where a conflict over land stood at the beginning of the escalation, most current intergroup armed conflicts in many parts of the Eastern Highlands Province are primarily triggered by sorcery accusations. Uneven economic development and disparities in the provision of infrastructure—such as roads, schools, and health facilities—compound the situation, as people now often attribute unexplained deaths to envious sorcerers from more remote and economically disadvantaged communities (Schwörer 2017). These conflicts cannot be attributed to sorcery alone, however. Wars typically emerge from long-standing tensions and animosities between local groups, which in turn fuel prejudices that both groups form about each other. As Helbling (2021: 17–18) explains in his theory of tribal warfare, most people would nevertheless prefer to settle conflicts peacefully, given the risks and costs of war. But when state institutions regulating and settling conflicts are either inefficient or absent, local groups find themselves in a security dilemma. In this situation, a conciliatory attitude can even be seen as a weakness, inciting a preemptive attack. It is thus only when peaceful conflict resolution through existing judicial forums fails that prejudices and fears about the potential violence of the other group take over and violence becomes the ultimate outcome.

Conclusion

As we have seen, the social organization of the Eastern Highlands in Papua New Guinea is characterized by remarkable flexibility and fluidity, challenging traditional anthropological models that fail to capture the diverse and dynamic nature of Highland societies. Despite the fluidity and impermanence of local groups, the constant interaction between neighboring communities, and their cultural and linguistic similarities, people from local groups in the Eastern Highlands continue to view one another as fundamentally distinct. This paradox stems from the deeply localized identities shaped by the unique environments, practices, and histories of each community. The land itself, with its magical and symbolic properties, becomes a defining factor in naturalizing and distinguishing local groups from one another. And these distinctions, though tenuous, provide fertile ground for prejudice to emerge, particularly in the context of conflict.

Prejudice in the Eastern Highlands of Papua New Guinea is thus not a timeless, static, or universal phenomenon, but dynamic and context specific, contingent on social relations, historical grievances, power dynamics and shifting alliances, competition over resources, and deep-seated fears—particularly fears related to supernatural harm such as sorcery. Accusations of sorcery, as we have seen, are a key expression of distrust and hostility, often directed at weaker or historically antagonistic groups. Such prejudices are not fixed, however; they adapt as alliances are forged or broken, as communities interact, and as perceptions of inferiority or equality shift. The violent conflicts between members of the Tapo and Agarabi local groups underscore this fluid and contingent nature of prejudice. These eruptions of violence reveal how suspicions, fears, and prejudices can continue to ignite conflict, even among groups that outsiders might view as indistinguishable and that had coexisted peacefully for decades.

Ultimately, this case study invites us to reconsider our assumptions about ethnic conflict and prejudice, urging us to recognize their contingent nature and the social forces that shape them, especially in contexts of deep cultural and historical fluidity. By doing so, we hope to gain a deeper understanding of the underlying mechanisms that fuel intergroup conflict and the possibilities for fostering reconciliation and peace.

Baptisttown, Evansville (USA): A History of Racism

African Americans settled in Evansville in the early 1800s and established there a vibrant community in what is now the city's Fourth Ward located around Governor Street, Canal Street, and Lincoln Avenue. By 1900, this part of town would house nearly 54 percent of Evansville's Black population. During the 1880s, this area became known as Baptisttown, a derogatory term used by Evansville's White citizens due to the number of Baptist churches in the area, although the residents there included Methodists and Catholics. Commonly used then as a stereotypical term for African American communities, this name would later be seized by the local residents who converted it into an important part of their community's identity.

According to Evansville historian Darrel Bigham, "Evansville, the only urban area in the county, had 29,280 residents. Although the county had only 127 Black residents in 1860, by 1880 it led Indiana counties in proportion of blacks and was second only to Marion County [Indianapolis] in the size of its Black population, which numbered 3,819" (Bigham 1987: 120).

This neighborhood continued to thrive, becoming home to many historic churches, homes, and schools, each of which carries today the legacy and history of Baptisttown and its residents. Baptisttown sustained its character as a densely populated Black community for nearly a century.

In the Introduction to this book, prejudice was defined as *only seeing people, things, and events from your own point of view*. For this case study on Baptisttown, we will discuss the Bloody Race Riot of 1903 and Evansville and the Ku Klux Klan to examine both the intentional and socially enforced aspects of human prejudice. This case study concludes with a few observations about prejudice in America today that can be seen as paralleling these two Baptisttown examples in the history of Indiana and the United States.

The Bloody Race Riot of 1903

On Friday, July 3, 1903, Robert Lee (also known as Lee Brown), a Black Baptisttown resident, entered Ossenberg's Saloon at Tenth and Mulberry Street in Evansville, Indiana. Lee began an argument over a nickel glass of beer with an employee and fellow Baptisttown resident Thomas Berry.

As Lee left, he threatened physical violence against Berry and vowed to return. Scared, Berry called a White patrolman named Louis Massey for help. Massey hid in a doorway near the saloon, awaiting Lee's return. Once Massey spotted Lee, he went up behind him and placed his hand on Lee's shoulder, who then turned and shot the patrolman in the abdomen. Staggering, Massey released Lee's shoulder, returned fire, and hit Lee in the chest. After the gunfire, Lee fled the scene, and Massey fell to the ground.

Lee was captured a few blocks away at Jones Drug Store on Seventh and Oak. When news of the incident circulated around the city, groups of White men gathered and started calling for Lee to be lynched. Captain George Covey of the Evansville Police Department took the threat of lynching seriously, and moved Lee into the police station to await his trial.

The following day, Lee was arraigned in court on a charge of assault and battery with intent to kill. Lee admitted to shooting Massey, but noted he had no desire to kill him. His modified plea was not guilty, and Lee was transferred to the county jail to await trial on a $5,000 conditional bail. If Patrolman Massey died, Lee would not be freed under any amount of bail.

That midnight, Massey died in the hospital. Shortly afterward, Judge Louis O. Rasch of the Circuit Court of Vanderburgh County issued an order reconvening the grand jury. Outside the county jail, a large crowd of White men was gathering that attempted to lynch Lee. The men mounted a telephone pole on the front wheels of an axle taken from an old wagon to use as a battering ram. The limited space between the jail and the sheriff's residence, however, made the ram useless. Then a large sledgehammer and a chisel were brought to use instead, but the mob's attempts to break into the jail proved futile.

Captain Covey was then able to persuade those in the mob to leave. Anticipating another lynching attempt, however, Lee was taken to the Knox County in Vincennes, Indiana. Evansville officials believed the jail there provided sufficient protection for Lee, and Vincennes was far enough away to discourage any lynch mob.

On July 5, however, over thirty-five hundred White citizens assembled at the Evansville jail, unaware that Lee had been moved out of town (when they finally heard where he was, the mob either did not believe what they had been told or did not care). Groups of men also roamed the streets in search of Black citizens to terrorize. At the same time, a small number of Black citizens armed with revolvers, rifles, and axes, proceeded toward the jail. Meeting near there, the resulting confrontation led to a horrific battle in which many people were injured and shot.

As reports of Black retaliation reached the ears of the White mob, revenge was demanded. "To Baptisttown," was the cry; "Let's kill every Negro in town." Gun shops, hardware stores, and even a few pawn shops were looted for ammunition and weapons. The streets of Baptisttown were filled with fleeing Black citizens as the White mobs stormed the community.

On July 6, Mayor Charles Covert issued a proclamation closing all saloons and prohibiting both public congregations and the carrying of weapons. He permitted the chief of police to deputize a special force of as many as five hundred men to maintain law and order. After hearing about what was going on, Indiana Governor Winfield T. Durbin sent the National Guard to Evansville. Between the deputized men and these soldiers, in all possibly as many as twelve hundred men were mobilized to defend the city from what was happening.

However, by ten o'clock that night, a White crowd had gathered on Fourth Street near the jail and the courthouse. Several men broke through a line of soldiers stationed on Fourth Street, and gunfire erupted. It is not known which side fired first, but the encounter killed six people immediately and five more in the following days. At least fifty people were injured.

This was the last act of mob violence; this race riot was over. Troops remained in Evansville until July 10. Lee died from pneumonia and the gunshot wound he had received back on July 3. On August 2, his body was placed in a pine box and buried in an unmarked grave at Walnut Ridge Cemetery in Jeffersonville (Sprinkles 1973: 31–43).

In the aftermath of the riot, approximately several hundred Black citizens fled across the Ohio River to Henderson, Kentucky. A few hid for a while in fields and woods outside the city limits. Others moved to Princeton, Vincennes, Newburgh, and Terre Haute, Indiana. Some went as far as Indianapolis and Danville, Illinois, where tragically a riot and lynching followed a week after the Evansville incident.

This riot marked a low point in Evansville's race relations. Though little mention of what happened then can be found in books and newspapers from the years thereafter, what had occurred that July continued to haunt Evansville. For example, in December 1905, a Black man named Lee Williams was accused of assaulting a woman near Florida Street and Fulton Avenue. Although the woman protested that Williams could not be the assailant because the man who assaulted her was White, police insisted she was mistaken and arrested Williams.

Like the Bloody Race Riot of 1903, rumors spread through the city that mob justice would take care of Williams. Remembering the violence of

1903, Sheriff Chris Kratz quickly called in reinforcements and prohibited gatherings near the jail. Within two weeks, Williams was tried and found guilty. What happened to him afterward is unknown today.

Evansville and the Ku Klux Klan

There was a two-block stretch of Evansville called the Midway that was once the scene of many saloons and rooming houses offering prostitution on the upper floors and open gambling down below. The owners there were White politicians who worked to elect city administrators who would overlook the vice that was making undesirable newspaper headlines. The Midway was just around the corner downtown from city hall and the city police offices.

In the immediate post–World War I years, there was a statewide effort to make Indiana more "moral." A state prohibition law was passed in 1918 that led to Evansville becoming a "dry" city at a time when nearly every intersection there had a tavern on one of its corners. It is no surprise, therefore, that illegal alcohol was still widely available after the law was passed, including the Black areas of Baptisttown and the Midway. The city also had a well-established "red light" district in an area called High Street just west of the central business district. This area had at one time over twenty brothels and a number of the most dangerous saloons in Evansville. It was also an area where both Black people and White people owned homes—a rare occurrence.

It was in this urban environment of wide-open gambling and illegal bootlegging that a religious political leader, Dr. William French, sent a letter to the Grand Dragon of the Ku Klux Klan in Texas asking for help in restoring morality to this city being dragged into the abyss by non-Christian forces, as he put it. Thereafter, Evansville, became ground zero in the 1920s for the establishment of the Klan in Indiana (which by 1924 had over four hundred thousand statewide members). It is estimated that nearly 25 percent of the White male population in Evansville back then were in the Klan. According to various sources, Klan membership was a broad cross-section of males in the city, both professional men and blue-collar workers. The Klan's activities, however, were more dramatic than otherwise. There were marches through the Baptisttown neighborhood, but they were mainly just public "warnings."

In 1925, a Klansman, a former sheriff named Herbert Males became the Republican candidate for mayor. He won a decisive election victory that November. How? Due largely to Black votes in the ward, which was under the control then of a Black attorney named Ernest Tidrington, a corrupt local political "boss." Mayor Males went on to lead a scandal-ridden administration. In 1929, he was defeated for a second term, although Tidrington tried to hold the ward together for him.

The Past Is Prologue

"What's past is prologue" is a well-known saying taken from William Shakespeare's play *The Tempest* (Act 2, Scene 1). Although Shakespeare may have wanted those in the audience back then to understand that the past may lead to—and excuse—what happens in the present, nowadays these familiar words are generally thought to be more open-ended in their meaning: History sets the stage on which the present is performed.

At the entrance to the National Archives Building in Washington, DC, there is an outdoor sculpture of a seated woman, called *Present.* It was carved out of Indiana limestone and was created in 1935 by the artist Robert Ingersoll Aitken (1878–1949). The words "WHAT IS PAST IS PROLOGUE" were carved across the base of this allegorical work of art. There is a companion sculpture on the other side of the Archive's entrance called "Past." The words written there are "STUDY THE PAST."

During the Bloody Race Riot of 1903, the mob cry of "To Baptisttown . . . Let's kill every Negro in town" could be seen today as foreshadowing the terror felt by the ten thousand Haitians living in Evansville today (Keen 2025) when, on September 13, 2024, Donald J. Trump, then the former president of the United States, repeated racist claims about Haitians living in the neighboring state of Ohio:

> "In Springfield, Ohio, 20,000 illegal migrant Haitians have descended upon a town of 58,000 people, destroying their way of life. They've destroyed the place," Trump said during a rambling press conference at his golf course in Los Angeles. "People don't like to talk about it. Even the town doesn't like to talk about it, because it sounds so bad for the town. They live there . . . for years it was a great place. Safe. Nice. Now they have 20,000 and I actually heard today it's 32,000." (Levine 2024)

Trump went on to add: "We will do large deportations from Springfield, Ohio, large deportations. We're gonna get these people out. We're bringing them back to Venezuela," naming the wrong country.

On learning that Trump had said this, Gelina Mascoe, executive director of the Haitian Center in Evansville, canceled their annual Flag Day because she did not want to put the city's Haitian families at risk. "So no, we don't get to celebrate our culture. You won," she said. "We don't get to display the beauty that is our culture. We don't get to share that. Because you don't want us to?" (Loesch 2025).

In 2023, the city of Evansville won formal designation for the Baptisttown neighborhood on the National Register of Historic Places. It may be true as Shakespeare wrote that "the past is prologue," but unfortunately what has happened in the past can also be easily forgotten. If you do not know to look for it by name on the internet, the history of Baptisttown and racial segregation there in the past is almost impossible to learn about.

What has happened in the past may leave material evidence of what life was like "back then" as real and enduring as those two Indiana limestone sculptures outside the National Archives Building. Museums are repositories of such evidence (Terrell 1991a, 1991b). Museum exhibits and collections can thereby bear witness to the realities of the past that should not be forgotten or ignored.

The Evansville African American Museum (EAAM) is located on Sondra Matthews Way, in the former Lincoln Gardens apartment complex, which was built in 1938 under the Public Works Administration. Lincoln Gardens was one of two housing projects designated specifically for Black residents in Indiana, established as part of President Franklin D. Roosevelt's New Deal during the Great Depression. Despite segregation and the racist policies at that time, the construction of Lincoln Gardens marked the beginning of a new era of Black achievement in Evansville. The community in Baptisttown went on to develop over two hundred Black-owned businesses along Lincoln Avenue, the main street in front of the apartment complex, and the people living there were able to establish a vibrant community way of life.

In the 1960s, Lincoln Gardens and the Lincoln Avenue area of the city experienced significant decline in their Black populations and funding, primarily due to desegregation and a general lack of available financial support. By 1997, the City of Evansville was planning to raze Lincoln

Figure 3.3. Evansville African American Museum today. © Tory L. Schendel-Vyvoda

Gardens. However, Sondra Matthews, the owner of *Our Times Newspaper*—Evansville's only Black newspaper—and a resident of Lincoln Gardens, met with the Evansville Housing Authority to preserve as many of buildings there as possible. Matthews explained why. "The basis of our economic life was going to be torn down as well. I just thought that if this happens, our grandchildren will not know what we had, the life we lived in the Lincoln Gardens area. They would not know how successful and prosperous we were" ("Lincoln Gardens"). Her efforts were rewarded when she was granted ownership of a single building situated at the intersection of Lincoln Avenue and the former South Garvin Street, which was renamed Sondra Matthews Way in 2023.

The EAAM, opened in 2007, tells about local Black history from 1820 to the present. While textbooks may overlook this history, the EAAM's tours, exhibitions, and the preserved living quarters of the Lincoln Gardens inhabitants immerse visitors in the past of a community that has helped shape Evansville and the nation. The EAAM aims to build an inclusive and expansive local Black identity, and believes that learning about its complex history can help all who come through its entrance recognize how the past is more than just "over and done with."

The sculpture called *Present* at the National Archives is also known by another name. That name is *Future*.

Notes

1. American visitors involved in social justice issues who visited the Canal Zone often remarked on its striking similarities with the U.S. South. For example, NAACP President Arthur B. Spingarn (1940–1965) wrote to then U.S. President Franklin D. Roosevelt on September 16, 1941, to express his outrage at the Canal Zone's segregation (GWC, SCRBC, 63/10).
2. The British occupied Manila and Cavite in the Philippines in the eighteenth century for almost two years, between 1762 and 1764.
3. In contrast, people categorized as white could visit Panama simply by paying $150 and could prolong their stay without difficulty.

Conclusion

So What?

Figure 4.1. A racist poster during the 1866 Pennsylvania gubernatorial race attacking Republican support for black suffrage following the Civil War. Public domain, U.S. Library of Congress.

Decades ago, the social anthropologist Anthony (Tony) Wallace wrote insightfully about what people must share in common psychologically to live together socially. For Wallace, poets, novelists, dramatists, historians, and other humanists are likely to approach this question with a sense of tragedy (or humor). The paradox of being human seems so apparent to them. Despite the obvious importance of our being extremely social animals, individuals in our species are always partly alone in their motivations, "moving in a charmed circle of feelings and perceptions" they cannot completely share with any other human being (Wallace 1961: 130). For this reason, Wallace insisted that when scientists claim all of us, or at least all who are members of the same organized group, "must share a common panel of interests and motives (ideal states-of-affairs to which strong affects are attached), the humanist can only raise his eyebrows and smile a wry smile at the naivety of scientism."

We believe there is much to recommend Wallace's wry smile. But asking how far people must share the same interests, goals, and motivations to live and work successfully together presupposes that we know why we all have the interests, motives, and prejudices that we do have, for better or for worse.

In this final chapter, therefore, we want to lay out in a formal way what we have been saying not only about prejudice but about beliefs of all sorts and motivations.

The Logic of Belief

Countless words for countless generations have been spoken and written about what philosophers call *logic*, a word that can be defined as *a particular way of thinking, especially one that is reasonable and based on good judgment* ("thinking"). What is supposedly special about "being logical," rather than illogical, irrational, or absurd, is that unlike being prejudiced, being logical—at least according to traditional Western philosophy—implies that you are right, correct, and fully in touch with reality. *The logic of a conclusion or an argument is its quality of being correct and reasonable* ("logic"). When it comes, however, to understanding why all of us have prejudices and other beliefs that may or not be rational or reasonable, we think it is more appropriate to ask instead: What is the logic of belief?

Needless to say, answering this seemingly simple question is not easy to do. We have found it useful, even so, to see coming to believe in something as a series of five logical steps.

Figure 4.2. The logic of how beliefs are created in five steps. Step 1 – *Experience*: receiving sensory input from the world around you. Step 2 – *Recognize*: perceiving repeated patterning in the environment. Step 3 – *Categorize*: ordering and indexing this patterning. Step 4 – *Interpret*: making sense of the patterning we have come to believe is probably real enough to be worth keeping in mind. Step 5 – *Believe*: reaching conclusions about what is or isn't real, and whether or not to do something. 1: Oh, My Dots!, CC BY-ND 4.0. 2: Rawpixel, CC 1.0. 3: Public domain, Freep!k. 4: OpenMoji, CC BY-SA 4.0, via Wikimedia Commons. 5: Vectorportal.com, CC 4.0. © John Edward Terrell

Step 1: Experience

It is easy to believe that when we are awake, we are fully aware of what is happening around us. This common belief is wrong. What we are aware of is not what our senses are picking up, but what we are able to recognize in what our senses are reporting given what we have previously experienced. In short, our awareness of things, events, and people is not only selective, but our sense of what is "now" is also strongly biased by what is "past." Said another way, what we have experienced in the past filters what we can easily learn about in the present.

Step 2: Pattern Recognition

Pioneering experiments by the Russian scientist Ivan Pavlov in the last century were about how animals—most famously dogs—learn when dinner is served and other basic facts of life (Tully 2003). Since then, psychologists and others have often described the role played by what we have learned in the past that helps us stay alive in the present as being "conditioned" by what we already know about ourselves, other people, things, events, and about what has happened when we did A or B, this and that, or nothing at all (Galaj and Ranaldi 2021). There isn't a common word or label for the kind of memories up there in your brain making it possible for this important work of recognition to be done. The word that may be close enough to what is needed is the word *assumption*. Alternatively, some have suggested words and phrases such as "heuristics" and "System 1" (Kahneman 2011), but both are often used to talk about someone's convictions and beliefs as well as their acquired *working assumptions*.

Step 3: Categorize

Being aware of what is happening around us takes not only time but also energy—specifical, metabolic energy, the energy popularly called the *calories* available in the food we eat. Given how costly it is to run a brain, and despite the popular idea that our memories, like photographs, vividly capture all that we have experienced in life, our memories are normally only as detailed and "true to life" as they need to be to see us through from day to day (Allport 1954: 20; Eagleman 2011: 27–30, 54; Eagleman 2015: 56; Seger and Miller 2010). Rather than seeing our brains as attics filled full of old photographic images or high-fidelity recordings, the memories privately stored up there on our shoulders are more like an abstract artist's impressions of reality than faithful reproductions of the real thing (Graziano 2019).

Labeling memories either as impressions or as assumptions, however, may not convey clearly enough that memories are not just simplified pictures, so to speak, of particular people, things, and events. We use our memories to deal with the here and now—and with what we may be faced with in the future. They are not merely abstract or pretty pictures. They are maps and basic guidelines that we consult to get—both literally and figuratively speaking—from A to B and beyond.

This is why we favor calling memories like these the *categories of thought*.

Step 4: Interpret

Like all animals to one degree or another, we all must play an active role in managing what we do to stay alive and well. What are called our "powers of imagination" are not only the keys to understanding what is happening in the here and now. Imagination is also needed to decide how to deal with and even fear what may happen next. Nobody needs to be told, however, that our powers of imagination can run wild and take us down the proverbial garden path to where we don't want, or shouldn't want, to go.

Step 5: Believe

Back in the 1950s when Gordon Allport was writing about the nature of prejudice, Tony Wallace was dealing with an equally challenging issue. What can and must we do as individuals to survive and get along successfully with others of our kind? Nowadays, his way of writing about this issue may come across as stilted and remote. In keeping with the way popular back then of seeing the world and our place in it as an organized "system"—even as a "definite kind of organism"—Wallace believed that what we need to know about and understand are the "patterns of learned

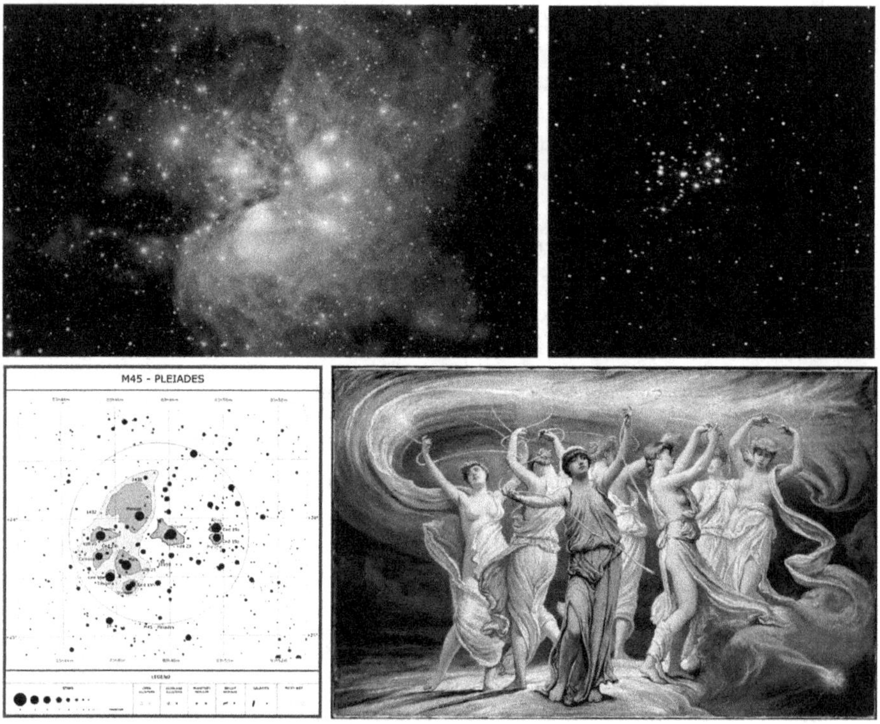

Figure 4.3. Our awareness of reality is always an interpretation of what actually exists. (top left) An astronomer's photograph of the Pleiades (M45). Antonio Ferretti & Attilio Bruzzone - Gruppo Astrofili Frentani, CC BY-SA 4.0, via Wikimedia Commons. (top right) The Pleiades as this part of the night sky can be seen with the naked eye. Sagesolar, CC BY 2.0, via Wikimedia Commons. (bottom left) A detailed drawing of the Pleiades from a southern perspective. Roberto Mura, CC BY-SA 3.0, via Wikimedia Commons. (bottom right) *The Pleiades* by Elihu Vedder (1884), a far more imaginative interpretation. Public domain, Metropolitan Museums of Art, New York. © John Edward Terrell

behavior" that different "parts" of the "social organism or system (individual persons and groups of persons) characteristically display" (Wallace 1956: 265).

> It is . . . necessary for every person in society to maintain a mental image of the society and its culture, as well as of his own body and its behavioral regularities, in order to act in ways which reduce stress at all levels of the system. The person does, in fact, maintain such an image. This mental image I have called "the mazeway," since as a model of the cell-body-personality-nature-culture-society system or field, organized by the individual's own experience, it includes perceptions

> of both the maze of physical objects of the environment (internal and external, human and nonhuman) and also of the ways in which this maze can be manipulated by the self and others in order to minimize stress. (266)

Wallace's use of the term "mazeway" never became popular in the social sciences. Even so, what he was writing about both then and now is of key importance: "the individual organism is conceived to maintain an extensive set of learned meanings. A mazeway—the organized totality of learned meanings maintained by an individual organism at a given time—is the cognitive map of the individual's private world regularly evoked by perceived or remembered stimuli" (Wallace 1961: 131).

Without claiming that the word we favor using rather than "mazeway" necessarily means exactly what Wallace took his chosen word to mean, we think the expression "what we believe" does a clearer job of expressing what all of us must do as "individual organisms" to survive and prosper. This definitely sounds better to us than "what we mazeway." Instead of *mazeways*, we favor writing about *beliefs*.

Consequential Beliefs

At the start of this book, we defined prejudice as *an assumption, claim, interpretation, categorization, labeling, etc. that is self-centered, inconsiderate, thoughtless, uncaring*. The shorter definition we gave this word at the close of that same chapter is more in keeping with what we have just said:

> Prejudice—*Only seeing people, things, and events from your own point of view.*

However defined, and however scientific you want to be in explaining what prejudice is or isn't, we are convinced that what needs to be studied and understood is why humans are so easily capable of turning our beliefs about other people into thoughts, feelings, and actions that may affect their lives and livelihood for worse—and yes, sometimes for better rather than worse. What needs to be explored is not Allport's "scientific problem" about what "the ethnic and psychological characteristics" of groups are (a question that takes it for granted there really are such things out there in the real world called groups). Instead, we need to ask: What do people do with their beliefs that are commonly called prejudices? And what are the consequences of what they have done?

Allport was well aware that our prejudices can have consequences not just for those having them but for others too. He was convinced, however, that "there is not the slightest justification for confusing the objective facts of prejudice with cultural or ethical judgment of these facts." As he bluntly insisted: "Whenever a negative attitude toward persons is sustained by a spurious overgeneralization we encounter the syndrome of prejudice. It is not essential that people deplore this syndrome. It has existed in all ages in every country. It constitutes a bona fide psychological problem. The degree of moral indignation engendered is irrelevant" (Allport 1954: 12). The luxury of the claim—or classification—that prejudices are just "spurious overgeneralizations" may have made sense decades ago. We have to wonder whether Allport would still hold such a dismissive view today. We would like to believe he would agree with us that pinning down the nature of prejudice calls for more than somehow proving that prejudices are simply false or ill-founded generalizations.

Regardless of whether or not he would agree, there is more to prejudice than just how right or wrong the opinions and beliefs commonly labeled as such may be. We are convinced that finding out what prejudices may do for someone having them calls for understanding the sequence, or series, of likely steps that may persuade any of us to think the worst (or sometimes even the best) about other people. With this end in mind, we have found it useful to say there are at least seven linked steps involved.

Step 1. ***Useful beliefs***: As we live our lives, what we come to believe and maybe even accept as true about other people, things, and events is often—perhaps more often than not—worth remembering because of the stories we are able to weave our beliefs into and then tell about them.

Step 2. ***Memorable stories***: The opinions and beliefs we have, and the stories we know and tell about them—both those that are completely fabricated and those that are accepted as unquestionably true (in which case, we often called them histories, recollections, and the like)—can help us flesh out and elaborate on the meanings and larger importance of what we have come to know and believe about the world and our rightful place in it (Terrell 1990).

Step 3. ***Instructive models***: Stories, fairy tales, novels, histories of this or that place, archaeological discoveries, and so forth can be used to help us merely pass the time during our waking hours, but even then—intentionally or unintentionally, consciously or not—what gets done by knowing and telling such stories can help us imagine (that is, *model*) what is possible, dangerous, heroic, or at least achievable "out there" in the world, for better or worse, if we set our powers of imagination to it (Terrell et al. 2023).

Step 4. ***Plausible explanations*****:** Stories, histories, and the like, used as models of what is possible or impossible, good or bad, and so forth, can help us understand and possibly explain why something happened in the past or might happen again in the future.

Step 5. ***Guidelines for control*****:** The old Latin proverb *Praemonitus, praemunitus*, "to be forewarned is to be forearmed," may be too negative a way of saying it, but being able to understand the past and foresee the future can help us decide how we may be able to control what may happen and why.

Step 6. ***Gaining control*****:** Having an apparently good sense of what may happen and what might be done to determine what does happen gives us a sense of empowerment and control.

Step 7. ***Empowerment and security*****:** Having a sense of control is not just empowering. Feeling this way can be reassuring and comforting. Prejudice can be a decidedly easy way to believe we truly know what to do, why to do it, and what will happen if we do.

Feeling thus empowered and confident about our own opinions, abilities, and beliefs would not be a challenging, even sometimes dangerous, human disability if our prejudices formed in this way were simply confined to our own personal likes and dislikes. Our history as a species, however, shows how easy it is for us to fall into the trap set for us by our human—and quite understandable—need to feel safe, secure, and in control. How is the line to be drawn between feeling confident and empowered, on one hand, and overconfident, self-centered, and basically selfish, on the other?

Is There a Solution?

Reading *The Nature of Prejudice* today over seven decades after it was written can be a sobering experience. Gordon Allport was apparently convinced that science—specifically, basic human rationality and the scientific study of human social relations—can overcome the limitations and undesirable side effects of being human (Allport 1954: xiv–xv, 85). He evidently believed that if we commit ourselves to the needed research work, we can become more rational, caring, and considerate creatures with the help of science. "Scientific laws are examples of rational categories. They are backed up by experience. Every event to which they pertain turns out in a certain way. Even if the laws are not 100 percent perfect, we consider them rational if they have a high probability of predicting a happening" (Allport 1954: 22).

His optimism must have been welcome news so soon after World War II. What about today? Given what is happening around the world now that we are well into the twenty-first century, it seems unnerving to read what he wrote so long ago about the victimization of minorities and the role of violence in human affairs, words that come across today as disturbingly timeless: "People have grown tired of their own inhibitions, and are reaching a state of explosion. They no longer feel that they can or should put up with unemployment, rising prices, humiliations, and bewilderment. Irrationalism comes to have a strong appeal. People distrust science, democracy, freedom. They agree that 'he who increaseth knowledge increaseth sorrow.' Down with intellectuals! Down with the minorities!" (1954: 58) If we had not told you these words were written over seventy years ago by an American social scientist, wouldn't it be easy for you to believe they are from an online social media post today by a political journalist, one of your worried friends, or a family relative?

As we remarked earlier in this chapter about the logic of belief, what we know and believe about ourselves, others, and the world around us cannot be based solely on what we ourselves have personally experienced for ourselves in life. Allport would have agreed with us that much of what we think we know is based on hearsay, social media, and the like. Therefore, both our personal prejudices and also what we labeled in Chapter 1 as our *social prejudices* collectively have a hard time living up to what Allport, conventional common sense, and popular belief alike would call being truly *rational* (Allport 1954: 27). However rational or not, it is not hard to understand why negative concerns and prejudices may often be widely shared socially.

What about *institutional prejudice*, which we defined in Chapter 1 as "what people are allowed to do by other people depending on how they are socially categorized and labeled"? Both personal and social prejudice involve categorization used mostly to define, identify, and decide what is "OK" or "not OK" when it comes to dealing with people, things, and events. Institutional prejudice, on the other hand, is when categorization of this sort is used, for instance, by the Taliban of Afghanistan to control other people and impose on them a set of rules, regulations, and requirements that they may or may not believe in or want to accept.

Is there a solution to this human dilemma called prejudice—specifically, institutional prejudice? Writing at the end of the first quarter of the current century, we find ourselves far from confident that our species can overcome its limitations as social creatures. It is worth remembering, nonetheless, that our assumptions and beliefs are not inherently true and correct. They can be genuine delusions. This is what, in everyday conversation, is called the "slippery slope" to failure, even self-destruction.

It may be hard for many of us to accept, but we are only human, not angels, gods, or advanced alien beings. Dealing with prejudice, therefore, means dealing with our weaknesses as a species as well as our obvious strengths.

For example, the consequences of being struck and killed by a rapidly moving train are real enough to explain why a warning sign got posted at Wilmcote, Warwickshire (Figure 4.4). Surely it isn't unreasonable to hope that everyone crossing those tracks believes in the wisdom of what is said on this public sign, and also isn't too distracted (or drunk) to ignore what could happen. However, simply putting up a sign saying "Stop Look Listen" does not keep anybody from doing the opposite. Nor is there any real way to control a swiftly moving train quickly enough to avoid such unfortunate "accidents."

The same holds for all our personal prejudices and our socially acquired fears and worries. To deal with our own prejudices and those of others, honoring the wisdom of popular sayings such as "facts matter" and "do unto others" may be a good place to begin, but such platitudes are all too often not good enough to do the job. Why not? Because history shows that honoring such simple wisdom can be hard for us humans to do.

Figure 4.4. Warning sign near Wilmcote, Warwickshire, England. Looking north along the Stratford to Birmingham railway line from the pedestrian crossing on the footpath to Pathlow. Stop Look Listen by David P. Howard, CC BY-SA 2.0, via Wikimedia Commons.

What's the point of challenging, after all, the convenience of the famous Duck Test? Or the obvious usefulness of an automated CAPTCHA asking you to prove you are a human being rather than a computer? Or what we have suggested can be called the Truth Test?

Much of the challenge, therefore, of dealing effectively with prejudice is that what any of us has in mind—what we believe either consciously or not—is *neurologically enabled*, *supported emotionally*, and may be both *intentional* and *socially enforced*. Furthermore, as we have seen in the United States involving the belief by some that the presidential election of 2020 was stolen from the Republican candidate, there is an abundance of evidence that beliefs can be strengthened by the repetition of the claims being made (Seitz 2022: 22).

What is the bottom line, therefore, of this perspective on what it takes to deal with prejudice? Confronting our prejudices must be both emotional and intentional. And to use a phrase more popular soon after World War II than it seems to be today, it must also be other-directed.

Key Points

1. Dealing with prejudice means dealing with our weaknesses as a species along with our obvious strengths.
2. Our prejudices are more than just our personal feelings or attitudes. They are our claims and beliefs about who gets to choose what can happen in life. They are why we believe such selectivity is right, proper, and entirely justifiable.
3. Much of the challenge of dealing with prejudice is that what we have in mind—what we believe either consciously or not—is *neurologically enabled*, *supported emotionally*, and may be both *intentional* and *socially supported*.
4. Instead of arguing about whether a prejudice is true or false, right or wrong, it makes more sense to ask whether its consequences are acceptable. If so, why?

References

Allport, Gordon W. 1954. *The Nature of Prejudice*. Cambridge, MA: Addison-Wesley Publishing Company.

Amnesty International. 2023. "Everything You Need to Know about Human Rights in Afghanistan 2020." *Amnesty International*. https://www.amnesty.org/en/location/asia-and-the-pacific/south-asia/afghanistan/report-afghanistan/.

Andrews, George Reid. 2004. *Afro-Latin America, 1800–2000*. 1st ed. New York: Oxford University Press.

Arango, Virginia. 1999. *La Inmigración Prohibida en Panamá y sus Prejuicios Raciales*. Panamá: PUBLIPAN.

Armbruster, Elif S. 2023. "The Racial Swamps of Reconstruction: Harriet Beecher Stowe's Life in Post-Civil War Florida." *Journal of International Women's Studies* 25(7), article 4. https://vc.bridgew.edu/cgi/viewcontent.cgi?article=3158&context=jiws.

"Asia's Dog Meat Trade." "Asia's Dog Meat Trade: FAQs." Downloaded on February 15, 2024. Humane Society International. https://www.hsi.org/news-resources/dog-meat-trade-faqs/.

Beck, Aaron. 1999. *Prisoners of Hate: The Cognitive Basis of Anger, Hostility, and Violence*. New York: HarperCollins.

Beer, Bettina. 2006. "Stonhet and Yelotop: Body Images, Physical Markers and Definitions of Ethnic Boundaries in Papua New Guinea." *Anthropological Forum* 16(2): 105–22. https://doi.org/10.1080/00664670600768284.

Bennett, Catherine. 2025. "Visit Afghanistan, Land of Culture, Cricket and Women Closeted in Their Own Homes." *The Guardian*, January 5, 2025. https://www.theguardian.com/commentisfree/2025/jan/05/visit-afghanistan-land-of-culture-cricket-and-women-closeted-in-their-own-homes.

Bergh, Robin and Mark J. Brandt. 2022. "Mapping Principal Dimensions of Prejudice in the United States." *Journal of Personality and Social Psychology* 123: 154–73. https://doi.org/10.1037/pspi0000360.

Berndt, Ronald M. 1971. "Political Structure in the Eastern Central Highlands of New Guinea." In *Politics in New Guinea*, ed. Ronald M. Berndt and Peter Lawrence, 381–423. Nedlands: University of Western Australia Press.

Billig, Michael. 2012. "The Notion of 'Prejudice': Some Rhetorical and Ideological Aspects." In *Beyond Prejudice: Extending the Social Psychology of Conflict, Inequality and Social Change*, ed. J. Dixon and M. Levine, 139–57. Cambridge University Press.

Bigham, Darrel E. 1987. *We Ask Only a Fair Trial: A History of the Black Community of Evansville, Indiana*. Bloomington: Indiana University Press.
Boyd, David J. 1996. "The Legacy of a Highlands Great Man." In *Work in Progress: Essays in New Guinea Highlands Ethnography in Honour of Paula Brown Glick*, ed. Hal Levine and Anton Ploeg, 43–61. Frankfurt/Main: Peter Lang.
Cohen, Esther. 1986. "Law, Folklore and Animal Lore." *Past & Present* 110: 6–37. https://www.jstor.org/stable/650647.
Corn, David. 2004. "The Safire Rules." *The Nation*, March 29, 2004. https://www.thenation.com/article/archive/safire-rules/.
Cushing, Mariah Terey. 2020. "Gadamer's Philosophical Concept of 'Prejudice' and its Use in Comparative Theology." *The Journal of Interreligious Studies* 29: 19–37. https://irstudies.org/index.php/jirs/article/download/423/467/.
Dennett, Daniel C. 1988. "When Philosophers Encounter Artificial Intelligence." *Daedalus* 117(1): 283–295. https://www.jstor.org/stable/20025148.
Dinerstein, Joel. 2009. "'Uncle Tom Is Dead!': Wright, Himes, and Ellison Lay a Mask to Rest." *African American Review* 43: 83–98. http://www.jstor.org/stable/27802564.
"Dog meat market." "The Dog and Cat Meat Trade in Southeast Asia: A Threat to Animals and People." Downloaded on August 30, 2023. https://media.4-paws.org/8/0/0/3/80039a8956751c7b9bf934c35993858592182db3/FOURPAWS_Big_DCMT_Report_GB.pdf.
Dovidio, John F., Peter Glick, and Laurie A. Rudman, eds. 2005. *On the Nature of Prejudice: Fifty Years After Allport*. Oxford: Blackwell.
Duberstein, Adam, Betz King, and Amy R. Johnson. 2023. "Pit Bulls and Prejudice." *The Humanistic Psychologist* 51: 183–88. https://doi.org/10.1037/hum0000259.
Duckitt, John, and Chris G. Sibley. 2017. "The Dual Process Motivational Model of Ideology and Prejudice." In *The Cambridge Handbook of the Psychology of Prejudice*, ed. Chris G. Sibley and Kate Fiona Barlow, 188–221. https://doi.org/10.1017/CBO9781316161579.
Durrani, Mamoon, and Kawoon Khamoosh. 2024. "A Child Bride Won the Right to Divorce - Now the Taliban Say It Doesn't Count." BBC News. September 29, 2024. https://www.bbc.com/news/articles/cx24evnk5d2o.
Eagleman, David. 2011. *Incognito: The Secret Lives of the Brain*. New York: Vintage Books.
Eagleman, David. 2015. *The Brain*. New York: Pantheon Books.
El Día. Carta de George Westerman. *El Día*, April 27, 1963 (GWC, SCRBC, 64/1).
Espinosa, Mariola. 2014. "The Question of Racial Immunity to Yellow Fever in History and Historiography." *Social Science History* 38: 437–53. https://doi.org/10.1017/ssh.2015.20.
Fair Observer. 2022. "What the Taliban's Constitution Means for Afghanistan." *Fair Observer*, January 26, 2022. https://www.fairobserver.com/region/central_south_asia/ikramuddin-kamil-afghanistan-constitution-taliban-news-afghan-world-news-43794/.

"fallacy." Stanford Encyclopedia of Philosophy. Downloaded on February 15, 2024. https://plato.stanford.edu/entries/fallacies/#NatFal.

Fiske, Susan T. 2012. "The Continuum Model and the Stereotype Content Model." In *Handbook of Theories of Social Psychology*, vol. 1, ed. Paul A. Van Lange, Arie W. Kruglanski, E. Tory Higgins, 267–88. Los Angeles: Sage Publications. https://psycnet.apa.org/doi/10.4135/9781446249215.n14.

Fonseca-Azevedo, Karina, and Suzana Herculano-Houzel. 2012. "Metabolic Constraint Imposes Tradeoff Between Body Size and Number of Brain Neurons in Human Evolution." *Proceedings of the National Academy of Sciences U.S.A.* 109 18571–76. https://doi.org/10.1073/pnas.1206390109.

Gaines, Stanley O., Jr., and Edward S. Reed. 1995. "Prejudice: From Allport to DuBois." *American Psychologist* 50: 96–103. https://psycnet.apa.org/doiLanding?doi=10.1037%2F0003-066X.50.2.96.

Galaj, Ewa, and Robert Ranaldi. 2021. "Neurobiology of Reward-Related Learning." *Neuroscience & Biobehavioral Reviews* 124: 224–34. https://doi.org/10.1016/j.neubiorev.2021.02.007.

Giménez-Fernández, Tamara, Dominique Kessel, Uxía Fernández-Folgueiras, Sabela Fondevila, Constantino Méndez-Bértolo, Nayamin Aceves, María José García-Rubio, Luis Carretié. 2020. "Prejudice Drives Exogenous Attention to Outgroups." *Social Cognitive and Affective Neuroscience* 15: 615–24. https://doi.org/10.1093/scan/nsaa087.

Graziano, Michael S. A. 2019. *Rethinking Consciousness: A Scientific Theory of Subjective Experience*. New York: W. W. Norton & Company.

Guerrón Montero, Carla. 2006. "Racial Democracy and Nationalism in Panama." *Ethnology* 45 (3): 209–28. https://doi.org/10.2307/20456595.

Guerrón Montero, Carla. 2012. "Black Is Not as Beautiful: Gender, Sexuality and Tourism in Panama." *Communication Papers: Media Literacy and Gender Studies* 1:10–23. https://raco.cat/index.php/communication/article/view/276446.

Guerrón Montero, Carla. 2020. *From Temporary Migrants to Permanent Attractions: Tourism, Cultural Heritage, and Afro-Antillean Identities in Panama*. Tuscaloosa: University of Alabama Press.

"GWC, SCRBC." Documents from the George Westerman Archive, George W. Westerman Papers, 1886–1988. Schomburg Center for Research in Black Culture, Manuscripts, Archives and Rare Books Division, Sc MG 505.

Hatfield, Gary. 2007. "The Passions of the Soul and Descartes's Machine Psychology." *Studies in History and Philosophy of Science* 38: 1–35. https://doi.org/10.1016/j.shpsa.2006.12.015.

Hatfield, Gary. 2017. "Descartes: New Thoughts on the Senses." *British Journal for the Philosophy of History* 25: 443–64. https://doi.org/10.1080/09608788.2016.1214908.

Hayano, David M. 1973. "Sorcery Death, Proximity, and the Perception of Out-Groups: The Tauna Awa of New Guinea." *Ethnology* 12(2): 179–91. https://doi.org/10.2307/3773345.

Hayano, David M. 1974. "Marriage, Alliance and Warfare: A View from the New Guinea Highlands." *American Ethnologist* 1(2): 281–93. https://doi.org/10.1525/ae.1974.1.2.02a00050.

Helbling, Jürg. 2021. "Pacification as Strategic Interaction of Indigenous Groups and State Actors." In *The Ending of Tribal Wars: Configurations and Processes of Pacification*, ed. Jürg Helbling and Tobias Schwörer, 8–55. New York: Routledge.

Hickey, Donald R. 1969. "The Prager Affair: A Study in Wartime Hysteria." *Journal of the Illinois State Historical Society* (1908-1984) 62(2): 117–34. http://www.jstor.org/stable/40191045.

Holyoak, Keith J., and Robert J. Morrison. 2011. "Thinking and Reasoning: A Reader's Guide." In *The Cambridge Handbook of Thinking and Reasoning*, ed. Keith J. Holyoak and Robert J. Morrison, 1–9. New York: Cambridge University Press. https://academic.oup.com/edited-volume/34559/chapter-abstract/293245852?redirectedFrom=fulltext.

Humans Rights Watch. n.d. "Background on Afghanistan: History of the War." https://www.hrw.org/legacy/backgrounder/asia/afghan-bck1023.pdf.

Ibáñez Castejón, Francisco Javier. 2021. "El Narrador en Panamá es una Tacita de Oro (1946) De Ricardo 'Fito' *Aguilera: Entre la Denuncia y el Prejuicio.*" *Cuadernos Nacionales* 29: 21–47. ISSN L 2644-4054.

"Indiana Crossroads: Hoosier Civil Rights." Digital Civil Rights Museum. Accessed June 26, 2025. https://www.digitalresearch.bsu.edu/digitalcivilrightsmuseum/items/show/111.

Jacob, François. 1977. "Evolution and Tinkering." *Science* 196: 1161–66. https://www.science.org/doi/10.1126/science.860134.

"judgment." Cambridge Dictionary. Downloaded on February 15, 2024. https://dictionary.cambridge.org/us/dictionary/english/judgment.

Jurado, Ramón. 1978. *Itinerario y Rumbo de la Novela Panameña: Tres Ensayos.* Panamá: Cultural Panameña.

Kahneman, Daniel. 2011. *Thinking, Fast and Slow*. New York: Farrar, Straus and Giroux.

Kanai, Akane, and Rosalind Gill. 2020. "Woke? Affect, Neoliberalism, Marginalised Identities and Consumer Culture." *New Formations* 102: 10–27. https://doi.org/10.3898/newf:102.01.2020.

Katz, Irwin. 1991. "Gordon Allport's 'The Nature of Prejudice.'" *Political Psychology* 12: 125–57. https://doi.org/10.2307/3791349.

Keen, Jodi. 2025. "A Call to Action." *Evansville Living Magazine*, January 23, 2025. https://www.evansvilleliving.com/the-world-is-here-gelina-mascoe/

Kelsey, D. M. 1890. *Stanley and the White Heroes in Africa Being an Edition from Mr. Stanley's Late Personal Writings on the Emin Pasha Relief Expedition and Discoveries in the Dark Continent, with Other Matter from the Works of His Companions and Predecessors, Including the Explorations and Adventures*. St. Louis and Philadelphia: Scammell & Company, Publishers. https://tile.loc.gov/storage-services/public/gdcmassbookdig/stanleywhitehero00kels/stanleywhitehero00kels.pdf.

Kenrick, Douglas T. 2012. "Evolutionary Theory and Human Social Behavior." In *Handbook of Theories of Social Psychology*, vol. 1, ed. Paul A. Van Lange, Arie W. Kruglanski, and E. Tory Higgins, 11–31. SAGE Publications, https://doi.org/10.4135/9781446249215.n2.

Kuku, Rebecca. 2021. "Police Warn of 'All-Out War' as Tribal Violence in Papua New Guinea Kills 19." *The Guardian*. April 21, 2021. https://www.theguardian.com/world/2021/apr/12/police-warn-of-whole-out-war-as-tribal-violence-in-papua-new-guinea-kills-19.

Kumar, Ruchi, and Zahra Joya. 2024. "Taliban Move to Ban Women Training as Nurses and Midwives 'an Outrageous Act of Ignorance.'" *The Guardian*. December 6, 2024. https://www.theguardian.com/global-development/2024/dec/06/taliban-afghanistan-ban-women-training-nurses-midwives-outrageous-act-ignorance-human-rights-healthcare.

Kuzawa, Christopher W., Harry T. Chuganic, Lawrence I. Grossman, Leonard Lipovich, Otto Muzik, Patrick R. Hof, Derek E. Wildman, Chet C. Sherwood, William R. Leonard, and Nicholas Langek. 2014. "Metabolic Costs and Evolutionary Implications of Human Brain Development." *Proceedings of the National Academy of Sciences* 111: 13010–15. www.pnas.org/cgi/doi/10.1073/pnas.1323099111.

La Estrella de Panamá. Carta de George Westerman. *La Estrella de Panamá*, April 27, 1963 (GWC, SCRBC, 64/1) [consulted at the Schomburg Center for Research in Black Culture, February 9, 2023].

Langer, Ellen. 1983. *The Psychology of Control*. Beverly Hills: Sage.

Langness, L. L. 1964. "Bena Bena Social Structure." Unpublished Ph.D. dissertation. Seattle: University of Washington. https://library.ucsd.edu/dc/object/bb0376657p.

Lasso, Marixa. 2013. "Nationalism and Immigrant Labor in a Tropical Enclave: The West Indians of Colón City, 1850-1936." *Citizenship Studies* 17: 551–65. https://doi.org/10.1080/13621025.2013.818370.

Lawn, Chris, and Niall Keane, N. 2011. *The Gadamer Dictionary*. London: A & C Black.

Levine, Robert S. 1992. "Uncle Tom's Cabin in Frederick Douglass' Paper: An Analysis of Reception." *American Literature* 64: 71–93. https://doi.org/10.2307/2927489.

Levine, Sam. 2024. "'They've Destroyed the Place': Trump Repeats Racist, Anti-Immigrant Lies." *The Guardian*, September 13, 2024. https://www.theguardian.com/us-news/2024/sep/13/trump-repeats-lies-haitian-immigrants.

"Lincoln Gardens." Digital Civil Rights Museum. Accessed July 23, 2025. https://www.digitalresearch.bsu.edu/digitalcivilrightsmuseum/items/show/56.

Lindenbaum, Shirley. 1979. *Kuru Sorcery: Disease and Danger in the New Guinea Highlands*. Palo Alto: Mayfield Publishing Company.

Lindenbaum, Shirley. 1981. "Images of the Sorcerer in Papua New Guinea." *Social Analysis* 8: 119–28. https://www.jstor.org/stable/23159562.

Linnell, John D. C., Ekaterina Kovtun, and Ive Rouart. 2021. "Wolf Attacks on Humans: An Update for 2002–2020." *NINA Report 1944*. Trondheim: Norwegian Institute for Nature Research. https://www.wwf.de/fileadmin/fm-wwf/Publikationen-PDF/Deutschland/Report-Wolf-attacks-2002-2020.pdf.

Loesch, Sarah. 2025. "Haitian Center Cancels Cultural Celebration as Impact of Ice Raids in Evansville Continues." *Courier & Press*, May 1, 2025. https://www.courierpress.com/story/news/local/2025/05/01/haitian-center-cancels-cultural-celebration-after-evansville-ice-raids/83366261007/.

"logic." Collins Dictionary. Downloaded on December 26, 2023. https://www.collinsdictionary.com/us/dictionary/english/logic.

Mergenthaler, Philipp, Ute Lindauer, Gerald A. Dienel, and Andreas Meisel. 2013. "Sugar for the Brain: The Role of Glucose in Physiological and Pathological Brain Function." *Trends in Neurosciences* 36: 587–97. https://doi.org/10.1016/j.tins.2013.07.001.

Náder Durango, Luz Ángela. 2020. "No Hay Nada que Extrañar o Recordar: La Destrucción del Tejido Social detrás de la Construcción del Canal de Panamá." *Muuch Xíimbal Caminemos Juntos* 5(10): 75–104.

Panama Tribune. 1940. "Varela Defends Cause." *The Panama Tribune*, November 30 [consulted at the Schomburg Center for Research in Black Culture, February 9, 2023].

Panama Tribune. 1958. "Raps Columnist Opposing Move to Ease Assimilation of Criollos." *The Panama Tribune*, October 19, 1 [consulted at the Schomburg Center for Research in Black Culture, February 9, 2023].

Pandey, Gyanendra. 2013. *A History of Prejudice: Race, Caste and Difference in India and the United States*. New York: Cambridge University Press.

Pettigrew, Thomas J., and Kerstin Hammann. 2014. "Gordon Willard Allport: The Nature of Prejudice." In *Klassiker der Sozialwissenshaften* (*Classics of Social Science*), ed. Samuel Salzborn, 174–8. Wiesbaden: Springer. https://link.springer.com/chapter/10.1007/978-3-658-13213-2_43.

"prejudice." Cambridge Dictionary. Downloaded on July 20, 2023. https://dictionary.cambridge.org/us/dictionary/english/prejudice.

Puyt, Richard, Finn Birger Lie, Frank Jan De Graaf, and Celeste PM Wilderom. 2020. "Origins of SWOT Analysis." *Academy of Management Proceedings*, vol. 2020(1): 17416. New York: Briarcliff Manor, NY 10510: Academy of Management.

Robbins, Sterling. 1982. *Auyana: Those Who Held onto Home*. Seattle: University of Washington Press.

Schmidt, Patrick L. 2022. *Harvard's Quixotic Pursuit of a New Science: The Rise and Fall of the Department of Social Relations*. Lanham, MD: Rowman & Littlefield.

Schulz, Richard. 1976. "Some Life and Death Consequences of Perceived Control." In *Cognition and Social Behavior*, ed. John S. Carroll and John W. Payne, 135–53. New York: Academic Press.

Schwartz, Earl Albert. 2002/2003. "The Lynching of Robert Prager, the United Mine Workers, and the Problems of Patriotism in 1918." *Journal of the Illinois State Historical Society* 95: 414–37. http://www.jstor.org/stable/40193598.

Schwörer, Tobias. 2017. "Sorcery and Warfare in the Eastern Highlands of Papua New Guinea." *Oceania* 87: 317–36. https://doi.org/10.1002/ocea.5173.

Schwörer, Tobias. 2020. "Ending War: Colonial Processes of Pacification and the Elimination of Warfare in the Eastern Highlands of Papua New Guinea." Lucerne: University of Lucerne. https://zenodo.org/record/3716138.

Schwörer, Tobias. 2021. "The Eastern Highlands of New Guinea (1930-1965)." In *The Ending of Tribal Wars: Configurations and Processes of Pacification*, ed. Jürg Helbling and Tobias Schwörer, 81–108. New York: Routledge.

Seger, Carol A., and Earl K Miller. 2010. "Category Learning in the Brain." *Annual Review of Neuroscience* 33: 203–19. https://doi.org/10.1146/annurev.neuro.051508.135546.

Seitz, Rüdiger J. 2022. "Beliefs: A Challenge in Neuropsychological Disorders." *Journal of Neuropsychology* 16: 21–37. https://doi.org/10.1111/jnp.12249.

Seitz, Rüdiger J., and Hans-Ferdinand Angel. 2020. "Belief Formation–A Driving Force for Brain Evolution." *Brain and Cognition* 140: 105548. https://doi.org/10.1016/j.bandc.2020.105548.

Seitz, Rüdiger J., Raymond F. Paloutzian, Hans-Ferdinand Angel. 2018. "From Believing to Belief: A General Theoretical Model." *Journal of Cognitive Neuroscience* 30: 1254C1264. https://doi.org/10.1162/jocn_a_01292.

Senior, Olive. 2014. *Dying to Better Themselves: West Indians and the Building of the Panama Canal*. Kingston: University of the West Indies Press.

Sibley, Charles, and Fiona Kate Barlow. 2017. *The Cambridge Handbook of the Psychology of Prejudice*. Cambridge University Press.

Siefkes, Christian. 2022. *Edible People: The Historical Consumption of Slaves and Foreigners and the Cannibalistic Trade in Human Flesh*. New York and Oxford: Berghahn Books.

Sigler, Thomas J., Kali-Ahset, Amen, and K. Angelique Dywer. 2014. "The Heterogeneous Isthmus: Transnationalism and Cultural Differentiation in Panama." *Bulletin of Latin American Research* 34: 229–44. https://doi.org/10.1111/blar.12266.

Sprinkles, Dallas. 1973. *The History of Evansville Blacks*. Evansville: Mid-America Enterprises Publication.

Swift, Jonathan. 1729. "A Modest Proposal for preventing the children of poor people in Ireland, from being a burden on their parents or country, and for making them beneficial to the publick." Project Gutenberg eBook. Downloaded on September 12, 2023. https://www.gutenberg.org/cache/epub/1080/pg1080-images.html.

Terrell, John. 1990. "Storytelling and Prehistory." *Archaeological Method and Theory* 2: 1–29. https://www.jstor.org/stable/20170203.

Terrell, John. 1991a. "Museums and Modern Life: 'Mirror for Man' or 'Door in the Wall'?" *Pacific Arts* 4: 8–13. https://www.jstor.org/stable/23409052.

Terrell, John Edward. 1991b. "We Want Our Treasures Back." *In the Field: The Bulletin of the Field Museum of Natural History*, March–April 1991. https://ia903406.us.archive.org/5/items/field62A/field62A_bw.pdf.

Terrell, John Edward. 2015. *A Talent for Friendship: Rediscovery of aa Remarkable Trait*. New York: Oxford University Press.

Terrell, Joh Edward. 2024. "Only Connect: The Challenge of Being Born Human." In *Family Beyond Family: The Varieties of Kinship Experience*, ed. Parker

Shipton and James P. Ito-Adler, 79–90. New York and Oxford: Berghahn Books. https://doi.org/10.3167/9781805397984.

Terrell, John Edward, and Gabriel Stowe Terrell. 2020. *Understanding the Human Mind: Why You Shouldn't Trust What Your Brain Is Telling You.* New York: Routledge.

Terrell, John, Mark Golitko, Helen Dawson, and Marc Kissel. 2023. *Modeling the Past: Archaeology, History, and Dynamic Networks.* New York and London: Berghahn Books. https://www.jstor.org/stable/jj.5501117.

Terrell, John, Eugene Anderson, Foreman Bandama, Abhik Ghosh, and Marcia Leenen-Young. 2025. *The Riddle of Intelligence: It's Not What You Think.* New York and Oxford: Berghahn Books.

"thinking." Cambridge Dictionary. Downloaded on February 18, 2024. https://dictionary.cambridge.org/us/dictionary/english/thinking.

"thought." Cambridge Dictionary. Downloaded on December 10, 2024. https://dictionary.cambridge.org/us/dictionary/english/thought.

Tristam, Pierre. n.d. "The Buddha Statues of Bamiyan, Afghanistan." About.com: Middle East Issues. Accessed February 14, 2009. https://web.archive.org/web/20090214194606/http:/middleeast.about.com/od/afghanista1/a/me080910.htm.

Tully, Tim. 2003. "Pavlov's Dogs." *Current Biology* 13 (4): R117–R119. https://doi.org/10.1016/S0960-9822(03)00066-6.

Tversky, Amos, and Daniel Kahneman. 1974. "Judgment under Uncertainty: Heuristics and Biases." *Science* 185: 1124–31. https://doi.org/10.1126/science.185.4157.1124.

van Rossum, Mark C. W. 2023. "Competitive Plasticity to Reduce the Energetic Costs of Learning." *bioRxiv* 2023.04.04.535544. https://doi.org/10.1101/2023.04.04.535544.

Villiers, Ambrosine. 1963. "Article Denunciation of Discriminatory Practices by Foreign Office of Panama." Panama City: Associated Negro Press [consulted at the Schomburg Center for Research in Black Culture, February 9, 2023].

Wallace, Anthony F. C. 1956. "Revitalization Movements." *American Anthropologist* 58: 264–81. https://www.jstor.org/stable/665488.

Wallace, Anthony F. C. 1961. "The Psychic Unity of Human Groups." In *Studying Personality Cross-Culturally*, ed. Bert Kaplan, 129–64. New York: Harper & Row, Publishers. https://www.taylorfrancis.com/chapters/edit/10.4324/9781315017990-58/psychic-unity-human-groups-anthony-wallace.

Watson, James B. 1983. *Tairora Culture.* Seattle: University of Washington Press.

Watson, James B. 1990. "Other People Do Other Things: Lamarckian Identities in Kainantu Subdistrict, Papua New Guinea." In *Cultural Identity and Ethnicity in the Pacific*, ed. Jocelyn Linnekin and Lin Poyer, 17–41. Honolulu: University of Hawai'i Press.

Westerman, George. n.d. "Attention to the Honorable Assistant Civilian Aide Mr. James C. Evans." GWC, SCRBC, 63/10 [consulted at the Schomburg Center for Research in Black Culture, February 9, 2023].

Westerman, George. 1949. "The Passing Review: Persons in High Places Still Profess Ignorance of W. I. Contribution." *The Panama Tribune*, June 19

[consulted at the Schomburg Center for Research in Black Culture, February 9, 2023].
Westerman, George. 1950. *A Minority Group in Panama (some Aspects of West Indian Life)*, 3rd ed. Panama: Nacional Civil League.
Westermark, George D. 1981. "Sorcery and Economic Change in Agarabi." *Social Analysis* 8: 89–100. https://www.jstor.org/stable/23159560.
Westermark, George D. 1984. "'Ol i Skulim Mipela': Contemporary Warfare in the Papua New Guinea Eastern Highlands." *Anthropological Quarterly* 57(4): 114–24. https://doi.org/10.2307/3317682.
Wilson, Carlos Guillermo. 1998. "The Caribbean: Marvelous Cradle-Hammock and Painful Cornucopia." In *Caribbean Creolization: Reflections on the Cultural Dynamics of Language, Literature, and Identity*, ed. Kathleen M. Balutansky and Marie-Agnes Sourieau, 36–43. Gainesville: University Press of Florida.

Index

www.ingramcontent.com/pod-product-compliance
Lightning Source LLC
LaVergne TN
LVHW050058140826
845500LV00029B/286
9781807581091